Praise for Strong Medicine...

Therapeutic for the soul. This book is filled with high energy and motivation. I would prescribe this book to anyone with a serious desire to find inner peace and realize the wonderful potential that we all possess.

Christopher Hennessey, M.D.
Internist
Deptford, NJ

Strong Medicine is a provocative and passionate book that provides helpful spiritual insight for those who are committed to walking with God in spite of life's difficulties.

Dr. Hunter writes from her heart as she shares from her personal experiences and faith struggles. She clearly reminds us that there is a cost with "the call."

The Rev. Elaine McCollins Flake, D.Min.
Co-Pastor, Allen A.M.E. Cathedral
Jamaica, New York

Dr. Hunter presents an extraordinarily creative book about how to live a successful life. She has an excellent writing style and a timely topic. That makes for a great book.

Keumsoon Hong, M.D.
Obstetrician Gynecologist
Philadelphia, PA

This book charts the course of moving from trauma to triumph. Dr. Hunter challenges us to grow and gives practical Bible-based suggestions to make it happen.

Dr. Franki Gibson
Psychologist and Author
In-Time Counseling, Inc.
Philadelphia, PA

Beyond the glamour of being an extraordinary success in ministry, there are the attacks of the enemy, who knows the value of your life in God and, more importantly, what you are doing for the Kingdom.

Dr. Millicent Hunter gives us an uncut version of it all in her own inimitable way. This book will bless you, encourage you, and give you the strength to be all that God has called you to be.

Dr. Cynthia Hale
Pastor, Ray of Hope Christian Church
Decatur, GA

Well, she has done it again. As with her other books, Dr. Millicent Hunter is able to put her writing finger on the very spiritual pulse of her readers. In *Strong Medicine,* she gets straight to the case of our conditions and provides prescriptions that actually work. This is a must-read book for people who are seeking sound advice and wisdom for their lingering conditions. To read this book is to be healed.

The Rev. Dr. Jessica Kendall Ingram
Adjunct Professor
Ashland Theological Seminary

All of us are eventually faced with unexpected events that can be difficult, and we search desperately for answers and solutions to them. *Strong Medicine: Prescriptions for Successful Living* provides practical, spiritual insights and direction, grounded in God's Word, that we all need on our spiritual journey.

The Rev. Dr. Jo Ann Browning
Co-Pastor, Ebenezer A.M.E. Church
Fort Washington, Maryland

Strong Medicine is mind stretching, relevant, and great reading. As a Christian physician, I will recommend this book to my patients as God's healing tool. This is a must read.

Phyllis Williams, M.D.
Heart Surgeon
Durham, North Carolina

Blessings
Dr. Millicent Hunter

STR●NG
MEDICINE

PRESCRIPTIONS FOR SUCCESSFUL LIVING

STR●NG
MEDICINE
PRESCRIPTIONS FOR SUCCESSFUL LIVING

DR.
MILLICENT HUNTER

W

WHITAKER
HOUSE

Editorial note:
The material in this book contains general guidelines and does not claim to be a substitute for seeking licensed professional counseling in the evaluation and treatment of specific spiritual, psychological, or medical problems.

At the cost of violating grammatical rules, we have chosen to capitalize the pronouns that refer to God, as well as His names and titles, and to lowercase the enemy's aliases, in order to give honor and glory to our God alone.

Unless otherwise indicated, all Scripture quotations are from the *New King James Version*, © 1979, 1980, 1982 by Thomas Nelson, Inc. Used by permission. All rights reserved.

Scripture quotations marked (KJV) are from the *King James Version* of the Bible.

Scripture quotations marked (NIV) are from the Holy Bible, *New International Version*, © 1973, 1978, 1984 by the International Bible Society. Used by permission.

Scripture quotations marked (TLB) are from *The Living Bible*, © 1971 by Tyndale House Publishers, Wheaton, Illinois. Used by permission.

STRONG MEDICINE

To contact Dr. Millicent Hunter:

Millicent Hunter Ministries   OR   The Baptist Worship Center
P.O. Box 5042   4790 James Street
Philadelphia, PA 19111   Philadelphia, PA 19137
1-800-MHM-1440   www.TheBaptistWorshipCenter.org

ISBN: 0-88368-660-0
Printed in the United States of America
© 2001 by Dr. Millicent Hunter

Whitaker House
30 Hunt Valley Circle
New Kensington, PA 15068

Library of Congress Cataloging-in-Publication Data

Hunter, Millicent, 1950–
   Strong medicine : prescriptions for successful living / Millicent Hunter.
      p. cm.
   ISBN 0-88368-660-0 (alk. paper)
   1. Christian life. 2. Suffering—Religious aspects—Christianity. I. Title.
   BV4501.3 .H86 2001
   248.8'6—dc21

                              2001001475

1 2 3 4 5 6 7 8 9 10 11 12 13 / 08 07 06 05 04 03 02 01

CONTENTS

This book is dedicated to my husband,
Dr. I. Marino Hunter,
whose love, support, and medical expertise
made this book possible.

* * * * *

I thank God for the gift
of my wonderful children,
Jason and Melissa.

Initial Consultation

God has an anointed prescription for healing your hurting heart—one that is guaranteed to work. Everyone has difficulties, sorrows, traumas, disappointments, and failures. Yet God has *strong medicine* and *prescriptions for successful living* that will overcome all your trials. My life is a test case of this truth. I have taken His cure and come into a healing and wholeness I never knew possible. When I find myself in a difficult situation—and I've had my share—I know I can count on God to use that situation for my good in His own time and way. He enables me to get around some brick walls, to go over others, and to go right through the rest.

Many Christians are confused about the nature and purpose of trials in their lives. At first glance, the Scriptures seem to contribute to this confusion. For instance, in John 10:10, Jesus said, *"I have come that they may have life, and that they may have it more abundantly."* Then, in John 16:33, our Lord seemed to say the opposite: *"In the world you will have tribulation."* There appears to be some ambiguity in these statements. Which is it? Do we have abundant life or tribulation?

The answer to this question is actually quite clear in the above Scriptures: the Christian life is a combination of *both* these experiences—and we can have them at the same time. Experiencing the abundant life doesn't mean that everything that happens to us is going to be good, comfortable, pleasant, and easy. Yet as believers and followers of the Lord Jesus Christ, and as recipients of His forgiveness, we can have the assurance that when tribulation comes, the Holy Spirit will be by our side to help us. Moreover, our greatest spiritual growth often comes through our trials.

Then how should we define the abundant life? It is God's "assurance policy" that, no matter what we may go through,

9

> ➢ Jesus has overcome the world (John 16:33).
> ➢ no weapon formed against us will prosper (Isaiah 54:17).
> ➢ all things will work together for our good (Romans 8:28).

God has granted the devil limited power and limited time to reign on this earth, for God's own purposes. Therefore, believers are not immune to the enemy's attacks. Every believer will face trials in this life, but God allows them for our good. When the Scriptures promise us, *"Everything you do shall prosper"* (Psalm 1:3), this does not mean that we are immune to difficulties. Neither is it a guarantee of perpetual health, wealth, and happiness. Rather, true prosperity is found in knowing God and living according to His Word. When God's wisdom is applied in our lives, it will bear good fruit that will build the kingdom of God. As a tree soaks up water and bears luscious fruit, we are to soak up God's Word, yielding actions and attitudes that honor Him.

The fallen world in which we live produces many kinds of tribulations—trials, illnesses, divorce, despair, addictions, poverty. In contrast, God produces in us the abundant life—His joy, strength, and holiness. He says, "I will take the total of your trouble and tribulation, your headaches and heartaches, your hurts and your stresses, your problems and your storms, and I will turn them around and use them for My glory and your good."

Because of God's promise to do this for you, you can have a new perspective on your trials. No matter what the situation in which you find yourself, God can work it out. He does so by providing you with His *strong medicine,* which you apply to your situation. His medicine is dispensed to you in the knowledge, wisdom, joy, peace, patience, and power He gives you in the midst of adversity. Just as a patient needs to follow doctor's orders and take all the prescribed medication in order to be cured of an ailment, if you follow God's Word and apply His "prescriptions" to all your hurts and sorrows, you will find healing, strength, and lifelong spiritual health. You will live a successful life—an *abundant* life—enjoying a closer relationship with your Lord than you ever thought possible.

—*Dr. Millicent Hunter*

1
TRAUMA UNIT
Critical Care for the Golden Hour

We were tearing through the streets, dodging traffic like a kid on a bumper car at an amusement park. It was nighttime, and the autumn air had cooled what was left of the warmth of an early October day. The street lights were bright, but not as bright as the lights in my head caused by a blinding, debilitating headache.

I didn't need this. I had never been sick a day in my life. I had never had an illness that an aspirin and a good night's sleep could not cure. This illness did not fit into my schedule. It was not on my "to do" list. There is really never a *good* time to be ill, but this had to be the *worst* time.

The ride to the hospital seemed endless. With my father at the wheel and my two small children in the backseat, I lay curled up in a fetal position in the front seat. Every stop light was a blur of color as we whizzed through the red lights, hoping to avoid a collision with another car.

LIFE'S UNEXPECTED TWISTS

I had never expected my life to be so messy. I had done all the right things, in the right ways, for the right reasons. Yet if a palm reader had studied my hand while I was growing up and told me that I would be married, then unmarried; start my life over alone with two young children; change careers; bury my mother, then six years later care for my terminally ill father until his demise; face a critical illness; pastor two churches; establish one church that would grow to two thousand members in three years; organize eleven churches in South Africa; and finally end up totally happy

11

and fulfilled with a wonderful husband and two beautiful children, I would have snatched my hand back, asked for a refund, and bolted out the nearest door, thinking that God must be punishing me for even considering the advice of a palm reader. If I had known what was coming, I would have felt that the price was too high to pay and the pain of each negative experience too great to bear.

As I lay curled up in pain in the front seat, I remembered my instruction from Lamaze class while preparing for the birth of my first child. I learned that one can lessen the feeling of pain if one focuses on something else at the first sign of discomfort. The short, rapid breaths were supposed to magically transform the excruciating pain of labor into a dull discomfort. So, as we raced to the hospital, I tried to take my attention off the pain I felt in my head. I tried to focus on something else—anything—hoping it would go away. However, the technique hadn't worked for me during labor, and it wasn't working now.

> IF I HAD KNOWN WHAT WAS COMING, I WOULD HAVE FELT THE PRICE WAS TOO HIGH TO PAY.

A VERY SERIOUS ILLNESS

We pulled up to the rear of the hospital. I don't know how I got into the emergency room, but minutes later I found myself lying on a bed in a small cubicle. A nurse was struggling to find a vein in my left arm strong enough to receive an intravenous needle. After failing several times, she hastily pulled the rubber tourniquet off my left arm and began slapping my right arm, trying to find a suitable site for the IV. Three doctors in starched white coats were huddled in a corner of that tight little room discussing the diagnosis and prognosis of my condition. I heard one physician say that he didn't know how I had been walking around functioning because my test results indicated that I had a very serious illness, and that it was in an advanced stage. The small cubicle where I lay became crowded with technicians and nurses asking me questions, looking into my eyes, poking me, and trying to take my vital signs. I ignored their questions and gave them my unspoken permission to do whatever they wanted to my body because I was too weak and too exhausted to respond.

THE THOUGHT OF DYING

Then I overheard one of the doctors make a statement that made me wish I had the physical strength to just get up and walk away from this dreadful situation. He said, "She probably won't make it through the night." My eyes filled up with tears at the thought of dying. I could not speak, so I began to utter words in my spirit. I thought about all the things God had promised me. I thought about all the things I had yet to do. Time seemed to stand still for me. One thought after another rolled through my mind. Every sermon I had ever preached about faith and every lesson I had ever taught about God's provision and healing came back to me. This was a time when I had to test every promise in God's Word. I knew that the Bible is clear—God is our refuge even in the face of total destruction. He is not merely a temporary retreat; He is our eternal refuge and can provide strength even in the face of death.

I didn't know what was causing my illness. However, I had overheard the doctors talking about my symptoms. There was inflammation around my brain, which is always a very serious diagnosis because it can be life-threatening. As I thought about this, I began to worry about the people who were under my care. I wondered, "Who will care for my children if I die? Who will take care of my young church, and how will the larger-than-life vision that God has given me for ministry come to fruition?" I knew that the world was not going to stop because I was sick, nor would all of these people and situations wait for me to get well before I could return to take care of them. How did such a devastating illness fit into the vision that God had given me and the work that I had yet to do?

AN UNEXPECTED ENEMY

When I first experienced the physical symptoms of my illness, I never thought about dying. The thought never crossed my mind that I could leave this earth at such a young age. Death was an enemy I had not faced before. This enemy casts the most frightening shadow over all our lives because we are the most helpless in its presence. We can struggle with many other enemies—pain, suffering, disease, injury—but we cannot wrestle with death. It has the final word.

I began to feel a flood of emotions. This was serious business. I was angry about being in a predicament that left me feeling so helpless and out of control of the situation. I just wanted to get away from it all. I wanted to get back to the business of leading and living and helping and building. Little did I know that this one catastrophic event would change the trajectory of my life.

What I did know was that I had been in tough situations before. I also knew that God has a way of custom-designing difficult circumstances in our lives in order to develop characteristics in us that transport us to the next level of relationship with Him and His blessings. Therefore, even though my body was paralyzed with pain, I sprang to my feet in the Spirit and said, *"I shall not die, but live"* (Psalm 118:17). My affirmation that God would use this difficult time in my life for His glory began the process of His working in the midst of my situation.

GOD USES DIFFICULT SITUATIONS FOR OUR GOOD.

TURNING POINT

I thought about all the books I had read and all the testimonies I had heard by people who could point to adversity or an intensive time of trial as the turning point in their lives. Their difficulties had propelled them to a place where their faith was deepened and strengthened. As a result, they were able to accomplish great things for God. I also thought about ministries that were having a tremendous impact on the lives of people for the cause of Christ. Invariably, the people behind those ministries had always come through a tremendous test, hardship, or extreme trial. Often, the greater the personal trials they had endured, the greater the impact they were having for Christ. The outcome of their lives showed me that any great anointing is generally accompanied by an intense time of trial and hardship.

I understood that our trials and hardships are necessary, for when we allow God to teach us through them, they produce in us patience and long-suffering, give us hearts of compassion, deepen our awareness of who God is in our lives, and bring us hope. They change our focus. They do not direct our focus to specific events and problems; instead, they show us how to keep our focus on God and His power in our lives at all costs.

WHAT HAVE YOU LEARNED FROM YOUR TRIALS?

Christlike characteristics are established in our lives as a result of our ability to come through painful and difficult situations victoriously. This is the process of growing and maturing that God has designed for us. Those who have never truly suffered may not appreciate God as much as those who have matured under hardship; those who have matured under hardship and seen God work in times of distress have a deeper insight into His loving-kindness and His plan.

I also knew that God promises us that all things work together for good for those who love Him, and that He always fulfills His Word. As I pondered these things, I concluded that this tremendous difficulty I was facing had to be a situation that would strengthen me for ministry, so that I, too, could have a greater impact on the lives of people for the cause of Christ. This gave me great hope.

BITTER PILLS

As I lay in the emergency room, my knowledge that this awful, untimely illness was a part of God's plan for my life was encouraging. Yet it was a hard pill to swallow! I knew that God had not caused my illness, but that He had allowed His "hedge of protection" to be removed for a season—for a purpose that I could not know at that time. Therefore, even though this sickness was like a bitter pill lodged in my throat, I knew God's purpose for it was a good one. My part was to trust Him. I had to live what I believed.

I began to quote every Scripture I could remember. The more I spoke God's Word in my spirit, the more determined I was to survive this current trial in my life. God's Word was like a "shot in the arm" to me because, although I was physically weakened by the illness, the Word of God was uplifting, energizing, and strengthening to my spirit. *That's strong medicine!*

Just hearing the Word reminded me of the power of God that was available to me. The Word was life to me, as it says in Psalm 119:50: *"Your word has given me life."* I knew that the Spirit of God was with me even during this very difficult time.

THERE ARE NO SURPRISES WITH GOD

Many times, the reasons for our trials are bewildering to us. I think I could have handled the shock of hearing that I had a life-threatening illness much better if I could have determined what had caused my condition. I am one of those people who take great care in keeping my surroundings clean and orderly. I always wash my hands before eating. When people cough and sneeze and don't cover their mouths, I become annoyed. I use paper towels to touch handles and doorknobs in public restrooms. I thought I had done all of the right things to avoid illness. Still, this sickness had somehow found me.

I had to come to grips with the fact that this was just "my time." Yet I knew that my illness was not a surprise to God. I knew that God was watching over me and directing every step that I was taking.

> The steps of a good [woman] are ordered by the
> LORD: and he delighteth in [her] way. Though [she]
> fall, [she] shall not be utterly cast down: for the LORD
> upholdeth [her] with his hand. I have been young,
> and now am old; yet have I not seen the righteous
> forsaken, nor [her] seed begging bread.
>
> (Psalm 37:23–25 KJV)

Our steps are ordered by the Lord. What a comfort it was for me to know that promise from God's Word during my unexpected and serious illness. God is fully in control, no matter what our circumstances.

An important truth to remember is that God never *causes* the evil that occurs in your life. Yet things do not just "happen" in the life of a believer. Your life is not an experiment. God is not managing your life through trial and error. After you are saved, God does not wonder what He is going to do with you now that you belong to Him. Every movement of your life is prepared and established by God Almighty. The way is made clear. This does not mean that you will never encounter difficulties. Neither does it mean that you live a robotic existence or that your life is predestined without regard to your personal choices or your own will. What it does mean is that when you give your life over to God, you put Him in charge.

GOD NEVER CAUSES EVIL.

When we are saved, we are saying, in effect, "Lord, I used to do my own thing, with little regard for anything or anybody. I did what I wanted to do. I went where I wanted to go, when I wanted to go, and I stayed as long as I wanted to stay. But now that I'm saved, Lord, I put You in charge. No longer my will, but Your will, be done." The same God who created life in you and saved you can be trusted with the details of your life.

> *As for God, His way is perfect; the word of the LORD is proven; He is a shield to all who trust in Him.*
> (Psalm 18:30)

It is not enough to accept Jesus Christ as Savior. We must also acknowledge Him as Lord. Acknowledging Christ as Lord involves making Him the ruler and controller of our lives. We yield, surrender, relinquish, give up, give over our own desires so that *God's will becomes our will.*

> *I delight to do Your will, O my God, and Your law is within my heart.* (Psalm 40:8)

17

For those of us who dislike any kind of control over our lives, this is not an easy thing to do. But the moment we ask Jesus to come into our lives, God puts a plan into action. He has a design for our lives, which He accomplishes through the working of the Holy Spirit. Yes, we might veer off the path or lose direction. We might go off on a tangent or find ourselves temporarily diverted, sidetracked, or detained. Adverse circumstances, such as illness, difficulties in relationships, loss, betrayal, and disappointment can throw us off course, especially if we are not prepared to respond to them. But, eventually, God will intervene in every situation and set our feet on the right course as we trust in Him.

SURPRISE ATTACK

Many Christians are unprepared for adversity because they do not realize that trials can come as the result of satanic attacks. Quite often his attacks surprise us. However, the Bible warns us to be on the watch for his assaults:

> Be sober, be vigilant; because your adversary the devil walks about like a roaring lion, seeking whom he may devour. Resist him, steadfast in the faith, knowing that the same sufferings are experienced by your brotherhood in the world. (1 Peter 5:8–9)

As a pastor, I often watch new Christians become discouraged because they mistakenly think their newfound faith makes them immune to satanic attack. They also believe they no longer need to worry about the old habits and sins that nearly destroyed their lives. The truth is quite to the contrary!

Ignorance is the devil's playground. When we are unaware of how satan operates, we can become his unwitting victims. In fact, we may not recognize his presence until his plan of destruction is well under way. We need to understand and anticipate his strategies and tactics.

WE LIVE IN A FALLEN WORLD

It is important to remember that not all our problems come *directly* as a result of satan's schemes. We can fall into trouble through our fleshly nature. It is true that when we accept Jesus Christ as Lord and Savior, we are no longer servants to sin. Paul said,

> *Knowing this, that our old man was crucified with Him, that the body of sin might be done away with, that we should no longer be slaves of sin. For he who has died has been freed from sin.* (Romans 6:6–7)

However, we must remember that we live in a fallen world. The battle between good and evil still rages on. John warned us about *"the lust of the flesh, the lust of the eyes, and the pride of life"* (1 John 2:16). Satan uses the weakness of our sinful nature to try to defeat us. Yes, even to the believer, satan still says, "Come." He reminds us of our faults, attacks our bodies and our emotions, and tempts us through fleshly desires.

SATAN TRIES TO CONVINCE US WE ARE DEFEATED.

Satan will tell us that we are defeated when we do something wrong. He tries to convince us that his works will always reign in us because our flesh is weak.

I am reminded of this truth when I think about an older gentleman in my congregation who struggles with a serious drug problem. His addiction began in his late teen years, and it has all but destroyed his life. It has led to chronic unemployment, homelessness, broken relationships, frequent hospitalizations, and a general feeling of hopelessness. My heart aches every time I pray with him and watch his eyes fill with tears as together we ask God to free him from this "demon" called addiction. He loves the Lord and cannot understand why satan continues to try to destroy his life. He once asked me during a counseling session, "Why doesn't the devil leave me alone? I thought that once I decided to come to Jesus, these old problems of addiction would leave me." I quickly reminded him that growth in God is a process, and that satan's goal is to try to bring down the kingdom of God in the lives of believers by tempting us through the power of the flesh.

THE POWER OF THE FLESH

Carnality, that is, being controlled by our fleshly nature, opens the door for the schemes or *"wiles"* of satan (Ephesians 6:11) to divert—and in some cases destroy—our witness for Christ. Satan's wiles are cunning devices that he uses with expert accuracy. The power of our flesh is no real match for the devil. Our warfare against him must be waged with spiritual weapons so that we can stand *"against principalities, against powers, against the rulers of the darkness of this age, against spiritual hosts of wickedness in the heavenly places"* (v. 12). We cannot defeat satan until we identify the ways in which he works in our lives and use the tools God has given us to defeat him. We must know his weapons, as well as the weapons given to us by the Spirit of God. (See Ephesians 6:10–18.) For instance, to use the *"shield of faith"* (v. 16), we must identify the direction from which the evil darts come toward us.

I tell the new Christians in my church that when they accept the Lord, satan does not cancel his plan of destruction for their lives. In fact, he accelerates that plan because, as believers, we are a greater threat to his kingdom. I encourage new Christians by reminding them that the power of God is always with the believer. It is important to remember that we must take an active, responsible role in maintaining the deliverance we have obtained in the areas of our lives where we are vulnerable—areas where we have struggled in the past. We become vulnerable in those areas when we do not utilize the power of God that is available to us. Jesus said that we would experience tribulation in this life, but that, even so, we are to be encouraged: *"In the world you will have tribulation; but be of good cheer, I have overcome the world"* (John 16:33). We are to be of good cheer. He overcame this world, and because He lives in us, we, too, will overcome.

WE PLAY A CRITICAL PART IN OUR BATTLES AGAINST SATAN.

As I counsel my parishioners, I tell them, "We play a critical part in the battles we wage against satan." Paul offered us some practical advice concerning this:

Present your bodies a living sacrifice, holy, accept-
able to God, which is your reasonable service. And
do not be conformed to this world, but be trans-
formed by the renewing of your mind, that you may
prove what is that good and acceptable and perfect
will of God. (Romans 12:1–2)

Have you let the devil pull you into some areas where you *know* you will be defeated? Are you presenting your life to God, or are you allowing it to be conformed to this world?

When Paul said that we are not to be conformed to the world but transformed by the renewing of our minds, he wasn't living in a fantasy world. He was no stranger to struggles against the flesh and the devil. In Romans 7:24, he cried out concerning these struggles, *"O wretched man that I am!"* In the same chapter, he also said, in essence, "The things that my spirit does not want to do, I find myself doing. The things I should do, I never accomplish. The devil has engaged me in battle, and I will never be able to win." (See Romans 7:18–19, 24.) Yet he knew this wasn't the whole story. He began to lift his eyes to another realm when he said, "Thanks be to God, I find my victory in Him." (See verse 25.)

Satan cunningly targets areas in our lives where he can use our fleshly desires to cause us to stumble. Christians must recognize his enticement and say, "This body is the temple of the Holy Spirit, and God can use it to manifest His glory and love. I will not partake of the corruption the world produces."

"Why Me?"

Many Christians may not realize it, but they often prevent God from working in the trials and difficulties of their lives when they fall into anger or self-pity and ask the question, "Why me?" Please understand that a heartfelt cry of "Why?" expressed to God in the midst of trouble is not wrong. God has compassion for our pain and bewilderment in these situations. However, when the question becomes one of resentment or accusation, we can block God's intervention in the adversities of our lives.

Things will happen in our lives over which we will have no control. During these times, we may be tempted to say things like:

"If God is a good God, why do I have to suffer?"

"Since I committed my life to the Lord, why have things gotten worse, not better?"

"Why do bad things happen to good people?"

"Why doesn't God just tell satan to 'back off'? I feel like a target."

Many believers have asked these questions over and over. They encounter one trial after another, just as Job did. (See Job 1–2.) Job might have been the most beleaguered person who ever lived, yet we can discover some crucial truths from his life that will help us during our own troubles.

THE TROUBLES OF JOB

Job, a righteous man who had been greatly blessed by the Lord, was a perfect target for satan's attacks. Satan went before God and said,

> *Does Job fear God for nothing? Have You not made a hedge around him, around his household, and around all that he has on every side? You have blessed the work of his hands, and his possessions have increased in the land. But now, stretch out Your hand and touch all that he has, and he will surely curse You to Your face!* (Job 1:9–11)

We can see that satan wanted to attack Job in order to challenge and mock God. However, we also learn from this passage that the devil couldn't act on his own. He had to ask God's permission to take away Job's wealth and children, and later his health. God limited satan's authority. He could not and still cannot exceed the limits that God sets: *"And the LORD said to Satan, 'Behold, all that he has is in your power; only do not lay a hand on his person'"* (v. 12).

As we consider the sufferings of Job, we need to keep in mind that, when God allowed satan to afflict Job, it wasn't because Job had sinned or "deserved" this treatment for anything he had done wrong. This wasn't some kind of punishment or revenge on God's part. Rather, God gave satan permission to afflict Job for the ultimate purpose of revealing His glory and demonstrating His power over satan. We see the same thing in the case of the man born blind mentioned in John 9. "[Jesus'] *disciples asked Him, saying, 'Rabbi, who sinned, this man or his parents, that he was born blind?' Jesus answered, 'Neither this man nor his parents sinned, but that the works of God should be revealed in him'*" (vv. 2–3).

Similarly, I had an assurance from the Lord that my illness was not a punishment. God allowed this sickness so that His glory could be manifested in my life and ministry.

GOD IS IN CONTROL

However, the sufferings of Job have much to say to us about our reactions to the trials and adversities of our own lives and how we allow them to affect our relationship with God. Satan attempted to drive a wedge between Job and God by trying to get Job to believe that, because of his suffering, God's governing of the world was unjust. The same temptation comes to us when we

GOD IS WORKING EVERYTHING OUT.

undergo trials. Because we know that God is the Creator and that He is in control of our lives, we can be quick to blame Him when things go wrong. Yet we must remember that when humankind rebelled against God and fell, sin entered our world, and many unfair and cruel things entered with it. They are the result of the human race's desire to live independently from God.

God continues to develop His character in us and to work out His purposes in our lives. However, He never forces His goodness on us. He allows us to retain our free will. In addition, even though *we* have turned our lives over to God and He is working out His purposes in us, He still allows other people to make their own decisions concerning whether or not to follow Him. If they continue to rebel against Him, then we and others may be affected by their ungodly actions. The evil that was unleashed at the Fall as well as contemporary humankind's rebellion against God continue to perpetuate evil and suffering on the earth. We live in a fallen world, where good behavior is not always rewarded and bad behavior is not always punished. When we see a notorious criminal prospering or an innocent child in pain, we say, "That is wrong!" Yes, it is. Sin has twisted justice and has made our world unpredictable and ugly.

Yet God is working in the midst of our fallen world. His plan for your life is often beyond your understanding, but you can trust that He is working out everything in your life for your good and His glory, no matter what you might be experiencing. Since God is in control, He will work all things out in His own time and in His own way.

The book of Job shows a good man suffering for no apparent reason. Sadly, our world is like that. But Job's story does not end in despair. Through Job's life we can see that faith in God is justified even when our situations look hopeless. (See Job 42.)

In light of this, the strength of our faith is an important factor in obtaining victory over adversity. Faith that is based only upon our receiving rewards or prosperity from God is not authentic faith. Authentic faith is strong and unshakable because it is built on the confidence that God knows what He is doing and that His ultimate purpose will come to pass—no matter what our circumstances. God is all-wise and all-powerful. His will is perfect, yet He does not always act in ways that we fully understand.

GOD HAS NOT ABANDONED US IN OUR SUFFERING

SATAN CANNOT ACT WITHOUT GOD'S PERMISSION.

Any person who is committed to God can expect satan's attacks. Satan hates God, and God's people as well. We are not exempt from trouble just because we love God. Although we may not be able to fully understand the pain we experience, our pain can lead us to discover a greater level of the power of God when we deepen our relationship with Him, since His power is made perfect in our weakness. He shows us how much He can strengthen us during these difficult times. We can go deeper,

24

farther, and higher in Him that we ever would have if we had not experienced the pain.

Sometimes believers may actually suffer more than unbelievers; they become satan's special targets. However, when we suffer, we must not conclude that God has abandoned us. He did not abandon Job. We must be willing to trust God in spite of our unanswered questions. When we suffer, we tend to trust God when we know the reasons for our suffering. However, if we always know the reasons why we suffer, then our faith does not have room to grow. Our faith grows when we trust God in spite of not having all the answers to our questions.

Remember that satan cannot move without God's permission. Also, God's power resides in God's people and can be used to overcome his attacks. Knowing this should cause us to remain close to the One who is greater than satan—God Himself.

BLAMING GOD

Satan and his evil forces are the agents of destruction—not God. The only sense in which God participates is through withholding His protection and delivering individuals over to the devil for His divine purpose. The book of Job plainly demonstrates this truth. Who destroyed Job's family and possessions and then afflicted Job's body? The answer is satan. Who gave permission for this to take place? The answer is God. (See Job 1:9–19; 2:4–7.)

This is, and always will be, the case in instances of affliction and destruction. God gives permission, but satan causes the actual occurrences of sickness, disease, or calamity. Then satan persuades humankind to think that God has brought these things to pass. Thus God is erroneously blamed by millions for the work of the devil, even by Christians who should know better. God merely grants His permission and uses the evil to work for the good of the righteous. If we do not understand that satan is the initiator and propagator of all wicked and evil things, a spirit of bitterness and anger against God can easily take root in us.

I remember visiting a parishioner early in my ministry who was in the hospital recovering from a stroke. The stroke had left him severely handicapped and almost unable to speak. I was very excited about visiting Deacon Jackson because I had such vivid memories of how he led the morning prayer before service each Sunday. He had a deep baritone voice that captured everyone's attention when he prayed out loud. He was a longstanding member of our church and a good deacon (I had known him since my childhood), and everyone admired him for his commitment and enthusiasm for the church and for God. I knew he would talk about "the goodness of Jesus and all that He's done for me" as he always did.

However, from the time that I arrived at his room until the visit ended one hour later, I felt captive. Despite his slurred speech and labored words, this good deacon and committed pillar of the church used what little strength he had to rail against God and to spew out his anger against God for *causing* his illness. Didn't he know that there is an enemy that opposes God and the people of God?

I have run across this type of harmful thinking quite often throughout my ministry—Christians blaming God for sickness, death, divorce, mental illness, crime, war, and all manner of evil. Satan must be having a good laugh.

God's withdrawal of His protection and giving satan permission to destroy is not the same thing as performing the destructive work. Satan destroys. God delivers.

SATAN'S PLAN, GOD'S PURPOSE

Satan plans destruction and ruin in the life of every believer. He wants to sabotage our good works, nullify our testimonies, and bring to waste every good deed that gives glory to God. God's purpose, however, is to build an intimate relationship with each one of us and to teach us how to destroy the works of the adversary. God will use any means necessary to draw us closer to Him. Therefore, He allows satan to continue his relentless assaults so that He may:

Rx *Develop character and faith in believers.* (See James 1:12; 1 Peter 1:3–16; 5:8–10; 2 Peter 1:4–10; Jude 20–24.)

26

Rx *Show believers the true level of their faith as they over-come adversity.* (See 1 John 2:13–14; 4:1–6; Revelation 2:7, 10–11, 17, 25–28; 3:5, 10–12, 21.)

Rx *Demonstrate the power of God over the power of satan.* (See Mark 16:17–20; 2 Corinthians 4:7–11; Ephesians 2:1–7; 3:10.)

Rx *Discipline people in order to bring them to repentance.* (See 1 Corinthians 5:1–7; 2 Corinthians 2:5–11; Job 33:14–30.)

PAUL'S THORN

For example, God allowed satan to afflict Paul in order to develop Paul's character and faith, and to demonstrate His power over the enemy. Paul wrote,

> *And lest I should be exalted above measure by the abundance of the revelations, a thorn in the flesh was given to me, a messenger of Satan to buffet me, lest I be exalted above measure. Concerning this thing I pleaded with the Lord three times that it might depart from me. And He said to me, "My grace is sufficient for you, for My strength is made perfect in weakness." Therefore most gladly I will rather boast in my infirmities, that the power of Christ may rest upon me. Therefore I take pleasure in infirmities, in reproaches, in needs, in persecutions, in distresses, for Christ's sake. For when I am weak, then I am strong.* (2 Corinthians 12:7–10)

We don't know what Paul's *"thorn in the flesh"* was, because he doesn't tell us. Some have suggested that it was malaria, epilepsy, or a disease of the eyes. Whatever it was, it may have been a chronic and debilitating physical problem that at times kept him from working. This thorn was a hindrance to his ministry, and Paul prayed for its removal. But God refused. The thorn kept Paul humble, reminded him of his need for constant contact with

GOD'S POWER SHOWS UP IN WEAK PEOPLE.

God, and benefited those around him as they saw God at work in his life.

Although God did not remove Paul's affliction, He promised to demonstrate His power in Paul. The fact that God's power shows up in weak people should give us courage. If we recognize our limitations, we will not congratulate ourselves for our accomplishments and victories, but we will continue to seek pathways of greater effectiveness in the work we are doing for the Lord. We must rely on God for our effectiveness rather than on simple energy, effort, or talent. Allowing God to work in the midst of our weaknesses not only helps to develop our character, but also deepens our worship, for in admitting our weaknesses, we affirm God's strength. When we are strong in abilities or resources, we are tempted to do God's work on our own, and that leads to pride. When we are weak, we allow God to fill us with His power. Then we are stronger than we ever could have been on our own. We must depend on God—for only work done in His power makes us effective for Him and has lasting value.

ON-THE-JOB TRAINING

My illness was a debilitating affliction. It was a test of my faith, my spiritual durability, and my knowledge of how to deal with satanic attack. God never tests us for the purpose of finding out how much faith we have. He is *fully aware* of our level of faith because He is *all-knowing.* Rather, our testing allows *us* to know more about the level of faith we have. Many of us think we have mountain-moving faith until a test comes along. Then the true level of our faith is revealed. Testing is for our benefit, not God's. Did I need more knowledge about how satan works? Yes! Did I need additional training? Yes! God used my affliction to provide on-the-job training for me in order to better equip me for the work that He had called me to do.

Christians who are serious about their walk and work for the Lord will encounter satan along the way. Therefore, we must be equipped with the knowledge to overcome him. Then we must learn to apply that knowledge in ways that will make us more effective as believers. Knowledge comes as a result of either experience or study. However, knowledge is not the same thing as wisdom. Understanding what is true,

28

right, or lasting—and exercising sound judgment—is wisdom, and true wisdom comes only from God. Wisdom is being able to look at life from God's perspective. Remember that God is more than willing to pour out His wisdom upon us. (See James 1:5.)

As we face great troubles, it is easy to focus on the pain rather than on our ultimate goal. Yet just as an athlete concentrates on the finish line and ignores discomfort while running in a race, we, too, must focus on the reward of our faith and the joy that lasts forever. Difficulties are never convenient. We have all faced problems that have caused us to want to walk away from them. It is easy to quit. However, rather than giving up, we must concentrate on developing our inner strength. *"That He would grant you, according to the riches of His glory, to be strengthened with might through His Spirit in the inner man"* (Ephesians 3:16). Instead of asking God for a "quick fix" or "immediate deliverance" from a difficult situation, we should ask Him, "What Christlike characteristic or quality do You want to develop in me?"

HIS PLAN INCLUDES "ALL THINGS"

As I faced my serious illness, I knew this was an opportunity for God to develop in me perseverance, endurance, and deeper faith. The Holy Spirit works to develop Christlike characteristics in us as we are yielded to His guidance. I was not going to allow this illness to interfere with my on-the-job training. This was my opportunity to deepen my commitment to Christ. I did not want the intensity of my present pain to cause me to miss what the Holy Spirit wanted to teach me.

Again, problems and human limitations have one great benefit: they give God the opportunity to demonstrate His great power. Therefore, I purposed in my heart not to resent this latest trouble, but to see it as an opportunity for God to develop something better and deeper in me.

God examines our situations and says, "I'm going to make them part of My plan." This does not mean that God's original plan is canceled out or that His plan changes. It simply means that anything and everything that happens to you, from the moment you accept Christ until the moment you die, God will work out for your good. Paul told us this in

Romans. *"And we know that all things work together for good to those who love God, to those who are the called according to His purpose"* (Romans 8:28).

For some Christians, this promise may seem hard to believe, because certain events happen in our lives that are so horrible we don't know how God could possibly use them for our good. Often, we would rather bury them in our memories than allow God to use them for our good and the good of others.

To illustrate this point, let me tell you about Michelle, one of the best youth workers at our church. She is able to minister to the young people in a very unique and powerful way because of a horrible event that took place in her life that left her broken and repentant. When she first came to me for counsel, Michelle was very distraught because she had been told that her sin was unforgivable. She was not a member of my church at that time, but I decided to counsel her anyway because she said she had no one else to turn to. At the counseling session, she began by telling me that, at the age of twenty, she had had an abortion. She was totally open and brutally honest about the circumstances that had led her to such a decision in her life. She never condoned her actions, nor did she excuse her wrongdoing.

SOME THINGS ARE SO HORRIBLE WE DON'T KNOW HOW GOD COULD POSSIBLY USE THEM.

I told Michelle that God works out *all* things—not just isolated incidents—for our good. I explained that this does not mean that all that happens to us is good. Evil is prevalent in our fallen world, and sometimes we make choices and decisions that are outside the will of God for our lives. However, when we give our situations over to God, confess our sins, and turn from our wrongdoing, God is able to turn around even the most horrible circumstances of our lives for our long-range good.

Michelle has a tremendous testimony about the forgiveness of God. As a result of experiencing the heartache of an ungodly relationship, a subsequent abortion, and then the healing power of God, she is able to relate to other young people and minister to them in a way that is life-changing.

"All things" really does include **all things**.

As I faced my illness, I felt that God was saying, *"Even this* can work out to be a blessing in My plan." I decided to hold God accountable to His Word. I had to trust that, in time, He would show me how to use this adversity in my life to His glory.

WAITING FOR GOD

When we look to God to work things out for His glory and our good, there are three important words we need to keep in mind: *in His time.* The "emergency room" experiences that we've been talking about in this chapter are circumstances that interrupt our lives, catch us off-guard, and stop us in our tracks. When these unplanned events occur, our otherwise normal routines go in a totally different direction, and our lives are never the same. There seems to be a domino effect as each new event triggers another event, and a series of changes takes place. During these times, we often have to wait out our circumstances, even as we are trusting God in the midst of them.

Waiting is the most difficult part of being in an emergency room. The feeling of a lack of control over events in our lives in itself produces anxiety. One is tempted to do something, *anything,* to try to understand and take control of the events that are taking place. No one wants to be a patient in an emergency room. No one volunteers for such an interruption in life. In the same way, we never think to volunteer for an "emergency room experience" in our spiritual lives because it means we have to wait on God for guidance and instruction—and that can be uncomfortable for us. We want to be in control.

The illness I was facing as I lay in the emergency room forced a change in my daily routine because it caught me off guard. I really struggled with it because what happened next would not depend on my choice and decision but on the doctor's decision and the outcome of my tests.

31

WHAT'S COMING NEXT?

Most of us experience a battle any time we face a significant change in our lives. The battle rages as we grope for the new and unfamiliar while still clinging to the old and familiar.

The day I ended up in the emergency room started out as normally as any other. I had my own plans and objectives. I had felt the dull pain of a chronic headache early that morning, but as women often do, I pressed past the pain and went about my business because I had work to do. Only ten hours later, I found myself a patient in an emergency room. My plans had been canceled, and my life was going in a totally unexpected direction. I had neither planned for nor expected these changes. Perhaps the most difficult aspects of change are our feelings of fear and stress from not knowing what's going to happen next.

THE MOST DIFFICULT ASPECTS OF CHANGE ARE FEAR AND UNCERTAINTY ABOUT OUR FUTURE.

Fear of change is a natural feeling. Habits and thought patterns developed over a lifetime are battle-resistant to change, and they do not give up easily. Satan will also try to sow seeds of hopelessness in our minds. He tries to destroy the work of God in us, but God speaks truth into our lives. His voice says that we have been created to be mighty overcomers. The same power that raised Jesus from the dead is resident in those of us who are believers. Jesus went to the cross so that through His redeeming grace we could have victory in situations that challenge us.

THE GOLDEN HOUR

When you are facing an emergency room experience, whether physically, mentally, emotionally, or spiritually, it's important to know how to respond to the shock of the change and pain you're experiencing. The sooner you can respond in a positive and life-giving way to your situation, the healthier you will be and the faster you will experience healing and growth.

In medicine, there is a term called the "Golden Hour." When someone experiences a trauma, the first sixty minutes can make the difference between the life or death of the patient. Usually, the first fifteen or twenty minutes are spent calling 911 and attending to the immediate physical needs of the patient. What happens next in the minutes that follow is crucial for the patient's survival. Many times, people have died in accidents, not because their injuries were so extensive, but because the proper emergency procedures were not implemented during that crucial first hour.

In a similar way, when we experience trauma, we immediately need to focus on God; His "emergency number" is prayer. God's power is available to transform us. Yet we must have the proper attitude and mindset when we first go to Him about the situation. The way in which we approach God in prayer is crucial to our receiving the help we need.

Rx Recognize that you are not alone.

Rx Surrender to His will.

Rx Open your heart to God's plan for your life.

Rx Allow God to work in mysterious ways.

RECOGNIZE THAT YOU ARE NOT ALONE

One of the most difficult aspects of change is the feeling of isolation. Many times depression accompanies change because we feel that we are "in this thing alone." God's Word promises that believers never have to fear aloneness in any situation. Jesus said, *"I will never leave you nor forsake you"* (Hebrews 13:5).

SURRENDER TO HIS WILL

When we find ourselves facing obstacles and difficult situations, many of us pray, "God, get me out of this!" If nothing happens immediately, then we pray, "God, *when* will I get out of this?" But what we ought to be praying is, "God, *what* should I get out of this?" There is purpose in trials and traumas. God does not *cause* problems to occur in our lives; nor does He plant obstacles in our way to keep us from reaching our goals and experiencing personal happiness. Rather, God often removes the "hedge of protection" from around His people in order to develop Christlike characteristics in them and to help them experience a deeper relationship with Him. As Joseph said to his brothers who had sold him into slavery, *"You meant evil against me; but God meant it for good"* (Genesis 50:20). Obstacles can be excellent teachers of spiritual lessons that we could learn in no other way. Therefore, we must surrender to God's will even when we do not understand God's plan and purpose for allowing certain events.

OPEN YOUR HEART TO GOD'S PLAN FOR YOUR LIFE

God always has a plan for our lives. Many times we do not see how difficult circumstances can be used in a positive way to carry out God's overall plan for us. But God does not see our lives as a series of episodes. God sees the bigger picture of the Christlike characteristics He wants to build in us through the challenges we face. Every difficult situation is ultimately designed to bless us. We should never allow depression to blind us from seeing an opportunity that God created or has allowed in order to bless us.

ALLOW GOD TO WORK IN MYSTERIOUS WAYS

Many times, when help does not come from the source we expect it to come from, we give up, as if God has only a few ways of answering our prayers. But God is very diverse. He has an unlimited supply of resources. He has many ways to give help, encouragement, and support to His people. Be open to allow God to bless you with the help you need from unexpected sources.

WE ARE IN GOD'S "LIFE SCHOOL"

The frustrations, trials, and traumas of life come to us to help us learn how to love God and follow Him more completely. We are all in a "life school." God designs the courses we take in this school, such as *faith, endurance, mercy, forgiveness, commitment, love,* and many more. When we look at life's negative experiences as a series of learning opportunities instead of things over which to become bitter and hopeless, we will have a positive perspective about our problems. We can look at these experiences as both God's preventive medicine and His healing prescriptions for a strong relationship with Him, which will give us a spiritually healthy and abundant life. When we are in the midst of our adversities, our difficulties may seem like bitter pills to swallow. But in the end, we will see that they are *strong medicine* for *successful living.* And through spiritual victory, we will enter into true life.

There were so many unplanned events and changes that took place in my life that October day. I had to seek God for strength to get through every hour because I did not know what each new minute would bring. But I settled myself into the life school of my present experience, excited about the prospect of what I would learn from God. If you find yourself faced with some unplanned events and challenges, pray this prayer of strength with me:

> *Lord, help me to know that You have an awesome plan for my life. Help me to open my heart to Your plan by surrendering my will to You. I accept these changes and challenges as an opportunity to know You in a deeper way. I know I am not alone; therefore, I yield to Your leading and guidance. Amen.*

Chapters one through five in this book will include "Spiritual Vitamins" essential to successful living as you face the challenges and changes that are inevitable in life. Just as vitamins are necessary to life, health, and growth, these "vitamins" are essential to your overall spiritual health and well-being, your relationship with God, and your growth in life as a believer. Take them faithfully to insure maximum spiritual health.

 SPIRITUAL VITAMINS

- ❏ Think about the changes and challenges you've faced in the last year or throughout your life. How have you responded to them? Have they drawn you closer to God or driven you away from Him?
- ❏ For the next week, pray the prayer at the end of chapter one, so that you will open your heart to God's plan for your life.
- ❏ Read and memorize these verses, so that you will know that God is with you and that you are never alone:

I will never leave you nor forsake you.
(Hebrews 13:5)

Lo, I am with you always, even to the end of the age.
(Matthew 28:20)

Have I not commanded you? Be strong and of good courage; do not be afraid, nor be dismayed, for the LORD your God is with you wherever you go.
(Joshua 1:9)

2

INTENSIVE CARE
Round-the-Clock Treatment

When I was in the emergency room, the doctors and technicians worked on me for about an hour, poking and prodding me and reading their instruments as they tried to determine the correct diagnosis for my illness. From time to time, I would glance at the clock on the wall; the numbers looked blurry to me. I could hear the constant clicking sound of the machine that was pumping medication into my body. These sights and sounds didn't bother me, however, because I knew that I was receiving the care I needed. Even with all my medical problems, I felt an overwhelming sense of physical comfort and well-being because I had committed my situation to God.

From the preliminary test results, the doctors believed I had spinal meningitis. A doctor leaned over the guardrail of my bed and assured me that I would be all right. I knew that. I had already claimed my healing. She told me that I was in one of the finest hospitals on the East Coast and that my condition, though somewhat rare, was easily manageable once it was brought under control. Yet I knew that it would not be the wisdom or expertise of the highly skilled personnel in that hospital that would ultimately heal me. It would be the *strong medicine* from the mind and heart of God that would bring healing, strength, and stability to my physical body—and my spiritual being, as well. God was working in my life through this latest trial, as He had in other trials and adversities I'd experienced in the past. There were many additional things He wanted to show me about Himself through this new experience, and I was ready for the challenge.

A SWEET TIME

After the doctors and technicians completed their tests, an orderly entered my cubicle to take me to a private room in the intensive care unit of the hospital. This room would become a sanctuary to me, where God would visit me and minister to me in an extraordinary way.

As I rode down what seemed like endless hallways and corridors, I heard the voices of people engaged in various conversations. But nothing in my surroundings was as real to me as the fact that God was working in my life. Wrapped in a hospital blanket like a butterfly in a cocoon, I was warm and confident that the Lord was preparing to do something very special in me. This was a sweet time for me because I knew that all I had to do was lie in my hospital bed relaxed and totally yielded to what God wanted to speak to my spirit.

I closed my eyes and pretended to be asleep. I sensed the worry and anxiety of my family members who had accompanied me to the hospital. Yet I no longer worried about who would care for my children or manage my home while I was away. I knew my children would be safe in His hands, as would I. I also had the assurance that God would make very good use of my time of rest and recuperation to teach me some important spiritual truths and to prepare me to serve Him in more extraordinary ways.

IN HIS HANDS

The orderly wheeled me into the room where I would spend the next ten days hooked up to machines. During that time, I was barely aware of my own physical existence, except when a nurse came to give me pain medication. I did not eat, watch television, or talk on the telephone. I just lay there with the emergency call button cradled in my hand.

The room was almost completely dark. The drapes were kept closed at all times because light causes unbearable pain to people with meningitis. Night and day seemed to blend together as God dealt with me. Yet even though I was given strong medications, my mind remained clear because I had the light of Jesus Christ illuminating my thoughts.

I was determined to fight for my life—physically and spiritually. I was determined to persevere and endure, knowing that if I did not, God's wonderful plan and purpose for me might never be realized.

ALONE WITH GOD

I was in intensive care all alone with God. God often allows us to be alone in certain situations so that, through them, we will have an opportunity to focus on Him. I felt that He had prescribed this time especially for me. You may also be alone —or feel alone—but God is all-sufficient for you. My stay in intensive care was such a spiritually blessed time that the lack of human contact didn't bother me. As I mentioned earlier, when I became ill, I was a single parent with two small children and was also pastoring a church. I had found it almost impossible to find any real time to be alone with God. Private time just didn't exist for me. So God used the downtime during my illness to get my attention and to draw me closer to Him.

> BEING ALONE IN CERTAIN SITUATIONS ALLOWS US TO FOCUS ON GOD.

I want to reemphasize here that God never *causes* a person to be ill just to get his or her attention. Again, we live in a fallen world where there are diseases and illnesses. But even though trials happen in life, God uses all things for our good. He uses our trials and tragedies to deepen our relationship with Him, because of His great love for us.

READY FOR THE BATTLE

During my stay in intensive care, God also described to me the magnitude of His plan for my life. I thought about His words continually, pondering what He was saying to me. Then God began to warn me of the seriousness of satan's strategy to interfere with His plan for my life. "What a great work God must have for me," I thought, "for satan to put forth so much effort to try to destroy me." The reality of satan's opposition and the battle I faced was another bitter pill to swallow. But swallow it I did, and postured myself for this test.

As we learned in chapter one, satan is our adversary. He is seeking to devour us (1 Peter 5:8). Right now he is either devising or carrying out a plan designed to cause our destruction. His strategies take a variety of forms as he plays on our fear, guilt, confusion, disillusionment, heartache, or physical distress. If his plans are successful, he will rejoice at our downfall. Nevertheless, we can take the wind out of his sails and dismantle every one of his wicked plans and devices through the power of God. Therefore, before we continue, I invite you to open your heart and spirit to the Lord as you pray this prayer with me:

> *Lord, pour out Your knowledge and wisdom upon me. Help me to see who satan is and how he works. I do not want to be his helpless victim. Teach me how to overcome him. Guide me through Your Word and speak to me in prayer. Amen.*

SPECIAL CARE NEEDED

When a person is experiencing a serious illness considered too critical to be attended to in a regular hospital ward, he or she is placed in intensive care in order to receive round-the-clock treatment. The condition is such that it requires the attention, the time, and the focus of medical experts. When I was in the emergency room, the doctors were not able to make a definitive diagnosis of my condition. They suspected that it was spinal meningitis, but I was not exhibiting all the symptoms of the disease, and certain test results had not yet come back from the lab. Unlike many people suffering from spinal meningitis, I had been functioning reasonably well before the pain became excruciating to me the evening I went to the emergency room. I had been working and going about my business. The diagnosis wasn't confirmed until the entire battery of test results came back a day or two after I entered the hospital. However, the doctors knew from the symptoms I presented that my illness was very serious. Therefore, I was placed in intensive care.

In intensive care, certain medical procedures are performed and certain medications are administered that cannot be dispensed in a regular hospital room because sophisticated equipment and more monitoring are needed. I was delighted to be placed in a specialized area of the hospital where I would receive the care of experts. I felt privileged because I knew that the concentrated efforts of the hospital's top staff were focused on the patients in that intensive care unit.

In addition to that, I had an excellent attending physician who oversaw all the activities of this staff. In intensive care, there are various medical personnel at different levels who address specific aspects of a patient's care. But the overall manager of a patient's treatment is the attending physician. He or she directs the care given by the nurses and technicians and the various departments that contribute to the care of the patient.

ALL OF US ENCOUNTER DIFFICULT LIFE ISSUES.

SPIRITUAL INTENSIVE CARE

All of us encounter painful life circumstances, permitted by God, that require the spiritual equivalent of the concentrated, highly specialized treatment one finds in an intensive care unit. Some of these life issues are:

- ➢ A troubled marriage or broken relationship
- ➢ Fear of failure
- ➢ Bitterness
- ➢ Unforgiveness
- ➢ Painful memories of the past
- ➢ Fear of the future
- ➢ Low self-esteem
- ➢ Illness
- ➢ Grief and loss

In order to grow in Christ and maintain inner strength and stability, we must exercise intensive care over our spiritual lives when we go through adversity. Painful life situations send us running to God's "emergency trauma unit" where He can care for us in a special way. They also cause us to focus our attention on the fractured areas in our lives that need to be addressed and healed. Just as a patient needing critical care receives the best that a medical facility has to offer, you and I can turn to God during difficult times and receive His loving, devoted care through our fellowship with Him, the ministry of the Holy Spirit, and encouragement from His Word. We should recognize that we are highly favored by God during our struggles because the concentrated efforts of the Holy Spirit are uniquely available to us. Just as a mother rushes to the side of her injured child, so God reaches out in loving urgency to meet our specific needs.

THE BEST CARE AVAILABLE

Being in a hospital intensive care unit can be a frightening experience, but when a patient knows he or she will

WE'RE IN THE BEST HANDS WHEN WE ARE IN GOD'S HANDS.

receive the best care the hospital has to offer, this is a great source of assurance. When I was in intensive care, I felt a sense of calm for a number of reasons. First, and most importantly, I knew God was with me. I also had confidence in the medical facility I was in, because it was the best hospital on the East Coast. I had exceptional doctors. In addition, I knew that I had an excellent insurance plan that would take care of all my special needs. When tragedy strikes, and you have insurance, you feel a certain relief because you know your expenses will be covered. As I will talk about more in a later chapter, God offers us an *assurance* plan that lets us know we're in good hands and that He is taking care of every detail. We're in the best hands when we are in God's hands.

RESTING IN THE MIDST OF UNCERTAINTY

As "patients" under God's specialized care, we can say, "I may not know what lies ahead, but I believe that it will be good, because God is an expert at healing and has my best interests in mind. Things may not have turned out the way I expected, but by faith, I believe that God is working out all things for my good, because He loves me and is involved in my situation." An attitude of resting in God's care is based on the belief, "I may not get what I ask for, but by faith I believe that what I receive will be good because God is good."

Hunters know that any kind of old dog will run after a rabbit as long as he can see it. But it takes a really good hunting dog to run a cold trail. That is what faith can be like. As Christians, we often have to run a "cold trail." We cannot see the Lord, we cannot see heaven, and we cannot always see when God is working in our lives, but we run on anyway with hope and faith. We base our hope and faith on God's loving nature and His faithfulness to His promises.

"For we walk by faith, not by sight" (2 Corinthians 5:7). As we go along, we should not be moved or influenced by what we see, because looks can be deceiving. What the devil intends for evil, God can always turn around for our good—and He will, if we allow Him to do so. In addition to not being moved by what we see, we also must not allow ourselves to be unduly influenced by what we hear or how we feel.

Just as it was for me, it will be the *strong medicine* that comes only from the mind and heart of God that will bring you healing, strength, and stability. Your first step is to acknowledge that God is working in your life through whatever trial you are experiencing, and that He wants to show you much about Himself through your situation. In the same way that the medicines we receive when we are sick attack our symptoms and ease our pain, when God uses an intensive care situation to enable us to grow, we will experience both change and comfort from His hand.

SPENDING TIME IN INTENSIVE CARE

Understanding what you can expect and what you should do during your intensive care time will help you gain the most benefit from it. This knowledge will enable you to cooperate with God in receiving new strength and spiritual growth through the difficult experience you are facing.

Round-the-Clock Care

In the intensive care unit of a hospital, a patient receives round-the-clock care with concentrated medical assistance.

43

As we give our circumstances over to God and allow Him to use them for our good, we are really giving ourselves over to God's round-the-clock care on our behalf. This is a time to truly *trust in His keeping power,* to *renew our commitment and love for Him,* and to *praise Him for His goodness and grace.*

Make a conscious decision to entrust yourself to God's keeping, and renew this decision whenever fear or anxiety returns to you. His love for you is immeasurable, and you can trust that He is steadily working on your behalf. This assurance will enable you to be ready for the challenge you are facing.

When I was in intensive care, I felt strong spiritually, even though I was weakened physically. However, sometimes, the routines and busyness of life can weaken our commitment to the Lord because we aren't focusing on Him and expressing our love for Him. A sudden trauma can bring things into focus for us, helping us to realize that we've grown apart from God. If this is your situation, use this time—when what is really important comes to the foreground in your life—to rededicate yourself to your Savior and Lord and to His purposes. He will bring newness and refreshing to your spirit as you draw close to Him.

The intensity of the trial may also cause you to ask the "Why, me?" question. Again, God honors our honest questions, but it's so important to guard against bitterness in such situations. Remember the elderly parishioner I talked about in chapter one? His faith seemed very strong until it was tested by a physical challenge. Yet Psalm 145:17 says, *"The LORD is righteous in all his ways and loving toward all he has made"* (NIV). Your hardest challenge may be to begin to praise God immediately when you experience a trial, but it is the best thing you can do. Praising God will lift you above your circumstance into the realm of God's love, power, and comfort.

When you do these three things—trust Him, renew your commitment, and praise Him—then you can rest in the knowledge of God's round-the-clock care and receive His ministry to you.

Our Attending Physician

As I mentioned earlier, in an intensive care unit, various medical personnel take care of the patient, but the overall care manager is the attending physician who gives direction to the hospital staff. Similarly, the Holy Spirit is our "Attending Physician" during our spiritual intensive care crises. He guides and directs others who are responsible for our spiritual care, such as teachers, preachers, and others who minister to us. However, the Holy Spirit is ultimately in charge of our teaching and training. He attends to us spiritually day and night.

> THE HOLY SPIRIT OVERSEES OUR SPIRITUAL CARE.

One of the names of the Holy Spirit is *Paraclete,* which literally means "one called alongside." The Greek word from which Paraclete comes, *parakletos,* may also be translated Advocate, Intercessor, Comforter, Counselor, and Helper. Although God is always with us, the Holy Spirit is called alongside us in a special way during our times of need. He is close by our side twenty-four hours a day. He is our Attending Physician in all our adversity, overseeing our spiritual care as we yield to Him.

Time to Be Alone

When I was in intensive care, I couldn't go home and I couldn't go to work at the church; I had to stay in the hospital until I was better. Yet this interruption in my life turned out to be the greatest blessing. The pain was alleviated because the doctors soon found the proper medicine for my condition, and I wasn't distressed by any physical discomfort. But I still needed to recuperate and regain my strength. All I could do was lie in my hospital bed, as I rested in God and yielded to what He wanted to speak to my spirit. Since I didn't have many visitors, I had plenty of time to pray and listen to God. This was a lonely time in the sense that there was very little human contact, but I don't remember *feeling* lonely because I was being spiritually blessed. The lack of

45

human contact didn't bother me and, in fact, was good for me at the time.

All of us need to be alone with the Lord in a quiet place on a regular basis, but especially when we experience situations that require intensive spiritual care. We tend to be able to hear from God better during times of solitude because we don't have the interference of people, commitments, and distracting environments. Your own intensive care experience is a time for you to get alone with God so that He can speak to you in His still, small voice—and *so that you can hear Him.* We won't all be in situations where this solitude is forced upon us. When you are facing adversity, you may have to *create* times for yourself where you can pause, get alone, and go to your secret prayer closet so that you can fellowship with God and hear His voice.

WE NEED TIMES WHEN WE ARE ALONE WITH GOD.

Downtime

Most of us live hurried, overscheduled lives. As a single mother and a pastor, my life was nonstop. However, I *had* to stop when I was admitted to the hospital. I actually welcomed this time because I was able to have uninterrupted fellowship with the Holy Spirit. Your "intensive care" situation may have forced you to cancel your plans and to slow down. Your priorities may have changed overnight. If not, it's important to slow down so that you can spiritually process what is happening to you. A slower pace helps us to take stock of our lives and to be ready to hear God when He speaks. It also gives us time to heal. So nourish your spirit during your downtime, so that you will be ready for action when God reveals the next step for your life.

During times of trial when we have to pull back, reevaluate, and refocus, we can feel as if we're wasting time. The opposite is true. God is saving us from lost time by getting our attention and setting us on the right path or on a new course He has planned for us.

When you begin to hear from God, you may receive words of comfort, encouragement, correction, or inspiration. But whatever you receive from God, know that it comes from your Father's heart of love, and that He is helping to clear out the obstacles in your life in order to make your paths straight in Him. Let this time be a sweet time for you, as it was for me, as you commune in your spirit with the Lord.

Fighting Infection

Sometimes a patient in intensive care can develop pneumonia. When we do not move around or breathe as deeply as normal, our lungs can fill with fluid, causing pneumonia. Also, a patient can be susceptible to other infections when the body's resistance has been lowered due to the primary illness. If the patient's physical strength and overall health are already compromised, a staph infection or hepatitis might set in because the immune system has been weakened. When a patient develops an infection that is secondary to the reason that he or she was admitted to the hospital, it usually means that either the patient or a hospital staff worker has not paid enough attention to cleanliness and sanitation. Pneumonia and other infections need to be treated before total healing can take place.

BITTERNESS AND ANGER AT GOD CAN RAGE LIKE AN INFECTION WITHIN US.

There is a spiritual analogy in this for us. Certain negative attitudes in our lives are like an infection or pneumonia that has set in and needs to be countered by *strong medicine*. Some of these attitudes are bitterness, unforgiveness, and underlying anger at God. Wrong attitudes can develop or deepen as we react to our troubles. It's very important to clear up these attitudes so that we can receive all the good the Lord wants to give us through our adversity. When we hold on to bitterness or unforgiveness, it can rage like an infection within us so that we are unable to hear God or move forward to the next step in His plan. Also, just as cleanliness is very important to preventing infection, keeping our hearts pure before God is crucial so that bitterness and unforgiveness do not make inroads into our lives.

47

As you rest in God's intensive care, confess your sins to Him and be set free from your guilt. Ask His forgiveness for your wrong attitudes, and forgive others who have wronged you. Release all the painful contents of your heart to Him so that you can find the joy and healing that God wants to give you in the midst of your situation.

Pray this prayer if you need an attitude adjustment:

> *Lord, I confess that my negative attitude interferes with my ability to clearly hear from You. I ask You to give me a pure heart and a forgiving spirit. Forgive me for my wrong attitudes, as I forgive others who have wronged me. I receive Your joy and healing right now. Amen.*

Need for Perseverance

I knew that I needed to persevere in my circumstances so that God's plan for my life would be realized. The same will be true for you in your trials. There will be such a temptation to give up! You may feel as if you're just keeping your head above water. But keep going! Things will get better. Determine to make it through your circumstance holding tightly to the hand of the Lord. You can receive comfort and encouragement from your Attending Physician as you keep close to Him.

Taking the Prescribed Medicine

Taking the prescribed medicine is a very important factor in a patient's recovery. We, too, have to take our "prescribed medicine"—to use the resources that God has given us to enable us to overcome. When I was in the hospital, it took a day or two before the doctors discovered the proper medication and pain reliever that would help me. We're very fortunate in that we already know the proper medicine for our spiritual needs: daily doses of the Word of God.

THE WORD IS GOD'S STRONG MEDICINE.

48

No matter how excellent the care may be, a patient needs to have a positive state of mind and must work with the doctor in order to receive the best treatment the physician has to offer. Likewise, God offers us the best of everything, but we have to be totally yielded to Him and take the "medicine" He has prescribed for us.

Patients are given intravenous treatments while they are in intensive care, so that much-needed medicine and nourishment can go straight to the source of their need. In the same way, we should continually read God's Word so that we can receive essential spiritual nourishment and strength. The Word of God is necessary to our intensive care experiences because it contains guidelines for applying God's *strong medicine* to the affected areas of our lives.

A BALM TO COMFORT

God's Word is a prescription for life. It is written instruction by the Great Physician for the preparation and administration of spiritual medicine. A steady intake of the Word of God is the best "intensive care" you can give your spirit. Jeremiah refers to the help God gives us as a *"balm"*: *"Is there no balm in Gilead, is there no physician there?"* (Jeremiah 8:22). A balm is a fragrant healing lotion or a soothing ointment. Its purpose is to gently comfort and soothe.

Even though our spiritual sickness may be very deep, it can still be cured. The cure may be applied even if we have brought our problems on ourselves. God can heal self-inflicted wounds, but He will not force His healing on us. Again, the patient has to agree to take the medicine if it is to be effective for healing.

FAITH COMES ALIVE AS WE APPLY SCRIPTURE

Faith is essential to both our recovery from adversity and further growth and maturity in the Lord. One of the reasons that the Word of God is so important is that faith comes alive at the point at which we apply Scripture to our lives. We need common sense and the desire to apply Scripture to those areas in our lives where we need help and healing. The

Bible is like medicine in that it goes to work only when we apply it to the affected areas. As we read and study the Bible, we must be on the alert for lessons, commands, solutions, remedies, and examples that relate to our life situations.

Now for some specific prescriptions. How does the Word of God help us during our recovery process and beyond?

THE WORD IS LIKE AN X RAY

First, the Word is like an X ray, helping us to clearly see the true nature of a situation. When a doctor holds an X ray up to a lighted screen, the cause of a patient's medical problem often becomes very apparent. An X ray is a tool that the physician uses in order to examine the body from an internal perspective. Because doctors are specifically trained to read the significance of the light and dark images on the film, they are able to spot problem areas in the human body that are not visible to the untrained eye.

If we were to observe a doctor looking at an X ray, it would become obvious to us that the light shining from the screen is necessary for the doctor to clearly see physical problems, such as fractures in bones and foreign masses in organs. In this life, we experience difficulties whose causes often lie beneath the surface of our understanding. But the Bible can be like an X ray to us, revealing these underlying causes. It illuminates the reasons for our brokenness, pain, trials, tribulations, and adversities. Study the Bible so that you can keep God's perspective in the midst of your situation.

A POWERFUL ILLUMINATOR

God's Word is a powerful illuminator, because the Bible is not a collection of stories, fables, opinion, or myths. It is not merely a book of humankind's ideas about God. Through the Holy Spirit, God revealed His person and plan to certain believers who wrote down His messages for His people. Although the writers used their own minds, talents, languages, and styles,

THE BIBLE IS COMPLETELY TRUSTWORTHY.

they wrote what God wanted them to write. Scripture is completely trustworthy because God was in control of its writing. Its words are entirely authoritative for our faith and lives. The Bible is *"God-breathed"* (2 Timothy 3:16 NIV). Therefore, read it and use it to illuminate your conduct and life.

One of God's characteristics is truthfulness. He embodies perfect truth, and therefore His Word cannot lie; it is true and dependable for guidance and help. The Bible is completely trustworthy. *"The entirety of Your word is truth, and every one of Your righteous judgments endures forever"* (Psalm 119:160).

A STRONG ANCHOR

Like ships at sea tossed by the waves, we feel the pressures of life push and pull at us, moving us to try anything to survive, even if it is wrong. The only sure way to stay afloat in the midst of such difficulty is to be anchored firmly in God's Word. God's Word makes us wise. True wisdom is not amassing knowledge, but *applying* knowledge in a life-changing way. Wisdom comes from allowing what God teaches us to make a difference in our lives.

A LIGHT THAT INCREASES

I find the Word of God phenomenal in that the more one reads and studies it, the brighter its light becomes. When I became a serious student of the Bible, I feared that my own lack of understanding would cause me to miss what God had for me. This taught me always to pray for guidance and wisdom when reading God's Word. A lofty, prestigious education is no substitute for simply asking God to illuminate your mind when studying His Word. "I don't understand what the words mean" is a common statement that I hear from people who are new in Christ or seriously studying the Word of God for the first time. I always try to encourage new students of the Word to be patient with themselves because any study of the Word of God must be conducted with both diligence and patience.

THE WORD IS LIKE A LONG-TERM HEALTH PLAN

We need to maintain our spiritual strength both during our difficulties and after we come through them. In the health field, a long-term health plan gives guidelines for living a healthy lifestyle, avoiding sickness, and maintaining overall physical fitness. Failure to follow this plan could result in serious physical consequences. The Bible is like a spiritual "long-term health plan" for us, giving us guidelines for living a godly life, avoiding sin, and remaining spiritually strong. If we ignore the plan, we may fall into temptation, make poor decisions, and risk our spiritual health.

THE WORD IS LIKE THE BODY'S DEFENSE SYSTEM

In order to defeat a disease, we must counteract its effects. The white blood cells in our bodies have been given to us by God to fight disease. Like frontline soldiers, they are the body's first defense. When you experience an injury, your white blood cells immediately go to the affected area to act as an inhibitor against further damage to that part of your body. For example, when a person fractures an ankle, white blood cells immediately rush to protect that area of the body. This protection appears to us as swelling, but it is actually the body building up a defense against further attack in that area. Similarly, God has given us His Word to enable us to counter satan's attacks and to protect us from further damage in our spiritual lives.

A Ready Soldier

When you read and study God's Word on a regular basis, you are like a soldier wielding a two-edged sword. This sword will jump into your hand when you need it to fight against temptation. You need to apply the Word of God to every difficult situation you encounter.

> *For the word of God is living and powerful, and sharper than any two-edged sword, piercing even to the division of soul and spirit, and of joints and marrow, and is a discerner of the thoughts and intents of the heart.* (Hebrews 4:12)

A Good Offense

Before the traumas of life strike you, allow God's Word to warn you. The best defense is a good offense. Knowing what God says about the subtlety of the enemy makes you privy to satan's devices. Study the Word of God to destroy the works of your enemy and bring about his surrender.

Jesus Himself challenged satan by quoting Deuteronomy 8:3, *"It is written, 'Man shall not live by bread alone, but by every word of God'"* (Luke 4:4). When you experience a traumatic situation, you can apply the Word like a potent medicine. You can remind yourself of these truths: *"He who is in* [me] *is greater than he who is in the world"* (1 John 4:4). "I am more than a conqueror through Him who loved me." (See Romans 8:37.) *"This is the day the LORD has made;* [I] *will rejoice and be glad in it"* (Psalm 118:24). *"The joy of the LORD is* [my] *strength"* (Nehemiah 8:10). "Let me not grow weary while doing good, for in due season I will reap if I do not lose heart." (See Galatians 6:9.)

> APPLY THE WORD LIKE A POTENT MEDICINE.

God's promises are completely dependable. There are literally hundreds of promises in the Word of God, and each one of them is worthy of our implicit trust. Yet if we are to trust the promises of God implicitly, what does that trust entail?

Trust, as defined by Webster, is "assured reliance on the character, ability, strength, or truth of someone or something." To trust God's promises, therefore, means that we rely with assurance on God's character, ability, strength, and truth as it is revealed to us in His Word. Storing God's Word in your heart and mind is a faith-builder. This knowledge alone should inspire you to want to memorize Scripture. But memorization alone will not keep you from fear, intimidation, and a lack of faith. You must put God's Word to work in your life.

AN EFFECTIVE PRESCRIPTION

The Bible is God's book and God's voice. In light of this, how do we put it to work in our everyday lives? Countless copies of Scripture sit unread on coffee tables, bookcases, and nightstands simply because people don't know how to read the Bible. What can you do to make God's Word real in your life? The clearest answer is found in the following words of Jesus: *"Ask, and it will be given to you; seek, and you will find; knock, and it will be opened to you"* (Matthew 7:7).

Ask

The first step in understanding the Bible is asking God to illuminate it for you. You should read the Word of God prayerfully. If anyone understands God's Word, it is because God has revealed its truths; it is not a result of the reader's own understanding.

Jesus promised the disciples that the Holy Spirit would help them remember what He had been teaching them. This promise underscores the validity of the New Testament. The disciples were eyewitnesses of Jesus' life and teachings, and as they were writing about these things, the Holy Spirit helped them remember the facts and truths of Jesus' life without taking away their individual perspectives. We can be confident that the Word of God is accurate.

> *Jesus answered and said to him, "If anyone loves Me, he will keep My word; and My Father will love him, and We will come to him and make Our home with him. He who does not love Me does not keep My words; and the word which you hear is not Mine but the Father's who sent Me. These things I have spoken to you while being present with you. But the Helper, the Holy Spirit, whom the Father will send in My name, He will teach you all things, and bring to your remembrance all things that I said to you."*
> (John 14:23–26)

Before reading the Bible, pray. Invite God to speak to you. Don't go to Scripture looking for your ideas, but go and search for His.

Seek

We should read the Bible not only prayerfully, but also carefully. *"Seek, and you will find"* (Matthew 7:7) is God's promise to you. The Bible is not a newspaper to be skimmed, but rather a mine to be quarried. Search for its truths like silver and gold, and hunt for them like hidden treasure. Then you will understand what it means to fear (respect) the Lord, and you will find that you know God. (See Proverbs 2:3–5.)

Any worthy discovery requires effort. The truths of the Bible are no exception. To understand the Bible, you don't have to be a brilliant scholar, but you must be willing to roll up your sleeves and work and search. We should build our lives on God's Word and build His Word into our lives, because the Word alone tells us how to live for Him and serve Him. Believers who ignore the Bible will certainly be ashamed at the Judgment. Consistent and diligent study of God's Word is vital. If we don't study the Bible, we will be lulled into neglecting God and our true purpose for living.

STUDY A LITTLE AT A TIME.

Here is a practical point. Study the Bible a little at a time. Hunger is not satisfied by eating twenty-one meals in one sitting once a week. The body needs a steady diet of physical food in order to remain strong. Likewise, the soul needs a steady diet of spiritual food in order to remain strong. When God sent food to His people in the wilderness, He did not provide loaves already made. Instead, in the morning, He sent them manna in the shape of thin flakes, *"as frost on the ground"* (Exodus 16:14).

God gave manna in limited portions; He sends spiritual food the same way. He opens the heavens with just enough nutrients for today's hunger. God provides a command here, a command there; a promise here, a promise there; a rule here, a rule there; a little lesson here, a little lesson there. Don't be discouraged if your reading reaps a small harvest. Some days, a lesser portion is all that is needed. What is important is to search every day for that day's message. A steady spiritual diet of God's Word over a lifetime builds a healthy soul and mind.

When my daughter returned home from her first day of school in the seventh grade, I said to her, "Did you learn anything today?" She answered, "Yes, a little, but I have to go back tomorrow and the next day and the next to learn more." Such is the case with learning the Word of God. Understanding comes little by little over a lifetime.

Knock

There is a third step to understanding the Bible. After the asking and the seeking comes the knocking. After you have asked and searched, then knock. In order to knock, you have to be standing at God's door—to make yourself available to learn what God wants to teach you through the study of His Word. You have to climb the steps, cross the landing, stand at the doorway, and volunteer.

Knocking goes beyond the realm of thinking and into the realm of acting. To knock is to ask: "What can I do?" "How can I obey?" "Where can I go?" It is one thing to know what to do; it is another thing to do it. But for those who do it, for those who choose to obey, a special reward awaits them. Those who are truly happy are those who both study and obey God's Word. Happiness comes to those who do what they read. If you read the recipe but never cook, you won't be fed. If you read the label on the medicine bottle but ignore the pills, you won't be helped. If you read the words of the Bible but never obey them, you'll never know the joy God has promised.

> IT IS ONE THING TO KNOW WHAT TO DO, AND ANOTHER THING TO DO IT.

APPLY WISDOM

Listen to counsel and receive instruction, that you may be wise in your latter days. (Proverbs 19:20)

In this age of information, knowledge is plentiful, but wisdom is scarce. Wisdom means more than simply knowing many things. It is a basic attitude that affects every aspect of one's life. The first step to wisdom is to fear the Lord—to honor and respect Him and to live in awe of His power (Psalm 11:10). The Bible is our standard for testing everything else that claims to be true. It is our safeguard against false teaching and our source of guidance for how we are to live. Paul told Timothy,

> *All Scripture is given by inspiration of God, and is profitable for doctrine, for reproof, for correction, for instruction in righteousness, that the man [woman] of God may be complete, thoroughly equipped for every good work.*　　　(2 Timothy 3:16–17)

God wants to show you what is true and to equip you to live for Him.

Again, the Bible is not a collection of merely human ideas about God. Through the Holy Spirit, God revealed His person and plan to certain believers, who wrote down God's message for His people. This process is known as inspiration.

> *Knowing this first, that no prophecy of Scripture is of any private interpretation, for prophecy never came by the will of man, but holy men of God spoke as they were moved by the Holy Spirit.*
> 　　　　　　　　　　　　　(2 Peter 1:20–21)

The Bible is God's very words that were given *through* people *to* people. The writers wrote from their own personal, historical, and cultural contexts, but they wrote what God wanted them to write. Scripture is entirely dependable for our faith and lives. We need to read it and use it as a guide for our conduct.

GOD'S TRUTH IS TIMELESS

Basic biblical principles and scriptural truths do not change. The details of difficult circumstances may change, but the wisdom to handle them properly never changes. Truth is timeless, and all truth is rooted in the Word of God. Truths about life are like oil in water. Drops of oil will remain unchanged despite the volume of water around them. The "oil" of God's Word works in the same way. The

Bible's stories and truths show us that the Word of God is relevant to today's crises and tragedies. In light of this, we can understand how crucial it is to saturate ourselves with God's Word if we are to live successful lives as believers.

SPECIFIC TO EVERY SITUATION

During your stay in the "intensive care unit," rest in the Lord. Listen to Him, wait on Him, and expect to get better. Read His Word. The Word of God is applicable to every situation that can happen in the life of a believer; it has been custom-designed for your need.

Pray this prayer for wisdom as you read and study the Word of God:

> *Lord, give me understanding and spiritual insight into the truths of Your Word. Help me to know that Your Word is true and relevant to my life and to the situations that confront me. Help me to apply Your Word to my life so that I may grow. I want to discover Your truth and become confident in my life and faith. Even if the truth hurts, I am willing to listen so that I can more fully obey You. Amen.*

 ## Spiritual Vitamins

❑ Think about your intensive care experience. Make time this week to get quiet before the Lord, hear His voice, and process what He is saying to you about your situation.

❑ For the next week, pray the prayer at the end of chapter two, to prepare yourself to receive all that God has for you as you read and study His Word.

❑ Read and memorize these verses, to remind yourself of the power of the Word and how you can apply the Word to specific difficulties in your life:

Your word is a lamp to my feet and a light to my path.
(Psalm 119:105)

The entirety of Your word is truth, and every one of Your righteous judgments endures forever.
(Psalm 119:160)

You, through Your commandments, make me wiser than my enemies.
(Psalm 119:98)

It is written, "Man shall not live by bread alone, but by every word of God."
(Luke 4:4)

3

DIAGNOSIS
Identifying Signs and Symptoms

I shuddered at the thought of having another needle inserted in my spine, but I knew I had to endure it if I was going to find out what was wrong with me. As the hospital orderly prepared to take me into the room where I would be given my *third* spinal tap in forty-eight hours, I prayed to God for strength. The pain of the spinal tap was overwhelming, but having the results of the procedure was crucial for the diagnosis of my disease and my subsequent recovery.

When I first arrived at the emergency room, the doctors examined me and ran preliminary tests to determine the cause of the excruciating headache from which I was suffering. Every procedure they performed gave them more information. The preliminary results pointed to spinal meningitis. However, some illnesses can mimic other diseases, and very specific tests were needed to confirm the diagnosis. Therefore, they continued to run tests for the next forty-eight hours. When they received the results from the final test, the doctors were able to make a diagnosis based on their findings of what the combined tests revealed; then they could say definitely, "This is spinal meningitis."

TREATMENT IS BASED ON DIAGNOSIS

Once my illness was fully diagnosed, the doctors knew what kind of treatment to give me and what type of medicine to prescribe that would most effectively address both my physical symptoms and the source of the problem. The earlier medication they had given me was intended mainly to ease my symptoms until a definite diagnosis could be made. However, when medications can directly target the root cause of one's illness and not just the symptoms, then they are more effective, and healing is more rapid.

TESTING UNCOVERS THE CAUSE

Diagnosing illnesses can be a guessing game at times, even for the best doctors. However, medical tests have been designed to help doctors link certain symptoms to particular diseases and maladies. Sometimes these tests seem more difficult for a patient to bear than the illness itself. In addition to the spinal taps, one of the tests I had to undergo was an MRI (magnetic resonance imaging), so that the doctors could check the inflammation caused by what they eventually confirmed was spinal meningitis.

Recently, open MRIs have become more common, but I underwent a closed MRI, where the patient is placed in a coffin-like machine. This experience was psychologically distressing because it was so confining. I had extreme claustrophobia as a result of lying inside such a small space. But I had to yield to the test so that the doctors could take the very deepest look at the problem—so that what was going on in the innermost parts of my physical being could be seen and examined. This test helped the doctors to make an accurate assessment of the problem and come to a conclusive diagnosis.

SPIRITUAL DIAGNOSIS

There is a spiritual parallel to this diagnostic process. We must determine the principal source of our traumas and troubles if we are to apply the appropriate spiritual medicine. You may be dealing with emotional trauma from a strained relationship with a spouse or child, physical trauma from illness, or financial trauma from debt.

WE NEED TO IDENTIFY THE SOURCE OF OUR TRIALS.

Whatever your particular trial, your solution lies in addressing its root cause and not just its symptoms.

The process of diagnosing the cause of your spiritual trial will sometimes be painful. However, this process is essential so that you may know the true source of your difficulty and respond to it in a healthy way. It is much better to yield to the difficulty of the testing. In this way, you can receive a correct diagnosis and apply the right medicine that will bring about more rapid spiritual healing.

There's an additional reason to seek a diagnosis for the source of our traumas. If we ignore our problems, hoping they will go away, they may become worse and cause further complications. If a person's leg has a small infection that is not properly cared for, it may worsen, so that the person ends up losing that leg to a more serious infection.

The way in which your health issues are diagnosed, addressed, and remedied will impact your future health. Likewise, your future spiritual health depends upon your submitting to God's testing, accepting His diagnosis, and responding in obedience to His plan of treatment.

IF YOU CAN FACE IT, GOD CAN FIX IT

People respond to adversity in various ways. Some bury their pain and busy themselves with life and work—essentially running away from the situation, like a person who ignores his symptoms and doesn't go to a doctor. Others obsess over the problem, turning it over and over in their minds and continually talking about it in a nonconstructive way. However, those who gain strength and wisdom through their experiences are able to acknowledge their situations, confront them, and then set out on a course to fix them—even if the process is painful to them.

The first two responses make it hard for us to receive the good that God wants to work in the midst of our adversities. But when we are willing to face our situations, entrusting them to God, then we allow God to use our circumstances for good, because we give Him something with which to work. We can then, under His guidance, take an honest look at our problems, accept a correct diagnosis, and receive strength to gain victory over adversity.

Diagnosis

"IMPOSSIBLE" PROBLEMS

An incident from the life of King David provides a good analogy of what happens when we are willing to face our difficulties. When David fought the giant named Goliath, champion of the fierce Philistine army, David was still just a boy. He tended sheep for his father Jesse, while his older brothers were fighting the Philistines as soldiers in King Saul's army. Jesse asked David to take supplies to his brothers and see how they were doing. When David arrived at the battlefield and began talking with his brothers, the giant stepped forward and boomed the same challenge to Israel that he had been making twice a day for over a month, *"I defy the armies of Israel this day; give me a man, that we may fight together"* (1 Samuel 17:10). The Israelites ran away in fright (running away from their difficulty), but David was indignant against Goliath and asked, *"Who is this uncircumcised Philistine, that he should defy the armies of the living God?"* (v. 26).

David's oldest brother rebuked him for his bold words, but David continued to make faith-based statements, until Saul sent for him. David could make these statements because he remembered all the other times he had faced "giant" situations in his life and God had made a way for him. He told Saul, "When I was taking care of my father's sheep, and a lion or a bear came and grabbed a lamb from the flock, I went after it with a club and took the lamb out of its mouth. That was God! Then, when it turned on me, I caught it by

WHAT A DIFFERENCE PERSPECTIVE MAKES.

the jaw and clubbed it to death. That also was God! I've done this to both lions and bears, and I'll do it to this heathen Philistine because he has defied the armies of the living God." Then he added this faith statement: "The same God who saved me from the teeth of the lion and the claws of the bear will save me from this Philistine giant."

Saul chided David, saying, "Don't be ridiculous. How can you fight a man like Goliath? You are only a boy, and Goliath has been in the army *since* he was a boy." (See 1 Samuel 17:1–37.)

63

PUTTING "GIANT" PROBLEMS IN PERSPECTIVE

Saul saw only a giant and a boy, but David saw a mortal man defying Almighty God. What a difference perspective makes!

David knew he would not be alone when he faced Goliath. He knew that God would fight for him, and so he looked at his situation from God's standpoint. When you look at an impossible situation from God's point of view, it helps to put giant problems into perspective.

David had a choice. He could have run from Goliath, or he could have stood and waited until the giant destroyed him. Instead, he faced his challenge head-on, armed with bold faith in God. From a natural standpoint, he was all alone when he faced Goliath. But in the Spirit, he was not alone, for God was with him.

The shepherd boy had a strong personal relationship with God, a history of other victories, and faith-building testimonies of how God can make a way when things look hopeless. Therefore, when he was challenged with having to face a giant, he was able to do it, because he had seen the power of God at work in his life.

THE BATTLE IS THE LORD'S

When Saul finally agreed to allow David to fight Goliath, he tried to give David his own armor to use. That was Saul's way of approaching the situation, but it was not David's way. Armed only with his shepherd's staff, his slingshot, and five smooth stones, he faced his enemy and said,

> *You come to me with a sword, with a spear, and with a javelin. But I come to you in the name of the LORD of hosts, the God of the armies of Israel, whom you have defied. This day the LORD will deliver you into my hand, and I will strike you and take your head from you. And this day I will give the carcasses of the camp of the Philistines to the birds of the air and the wild beasts of the earth, that all the earth may know that there is a God in Israel. Then all this assembly shall know that the LORD does not*

save with sword and spear; for the battle is the Lord's, and He will give you into our hands.

(1 Samuel 17:45–47)

Then David killed Goliath with just one stone that hit the giant squarely in the middle of his forehead. After the Philistine soldiers saw this, they all fled, but the Israelite army pursued them, prevailed over them, and plundered their goods. (See 1 Samuel 17:37–53.)

David knew something about the power of God. He knew that *"the battle is the Lord's."* You can be assured that the same power is available for you when you are confronted with a challenge. No matter what giants you are facing in your life—divorce, infidelity, betrayal, debt, addiction, unemployment, loneliness, sickness, depression, anger, unforgiveness, or bitterness—you have a choice.

THE LIVING GOD IS WITH YOU.

You can run from your Goliath, you can stay where you are and wait until it consumes you, or you can face it head-on—armed with an unwavering faith and trust in God, knowing that *"the battle is the Lord's."*

FACE YOUR DIFFICULTIES WITH FAITH

You might feel as if you're standing alone, but the living God is with you, and He will help you. Face your giant by maintaining a strong, personal relationship with the Lord and acknowledging what He has done to help you in past difficulties. Think of other victories God has given you and remind yourself of His power and strength in your life. If you struggle with having faith in God, read the twelfth chapter of Hebrews in order to build your faith.

FAITH TRUSTS GOD TO...
move mountains,
lift the burden,
supply the need,
perform the miracle,
conquer the enemy.

FAITH...
recognizes that God is,
acknowledges that God can,
knows that God loves,
understands that God cares,
believes that God saves,
confirms that God heals,
depends on God's promises,
relies on God's Spirit,
trusts in God's wisdom,
believes in God's Word,
leans on God's arm,
waits on God's time,
stays in God's will.

DIAGNOSIS PRECEDES TREATMENT

Once we make the decision to face our difficulties with faith, we are ready to diagnose their cause, under God's guidance. What exactly is a diagnosis? The dictionary gives several useful definitions:

➤ a recognition or identification of a disease by its signs and symptoms
➤ an investigation or analysis of the cause or nature of a condition, situation, or problem
➤ a statement or conclusion from such an analysis

We should keep in mind that diagnosis is not the same procedure as treatment. It *precedes* treatment. This is an important point, because when we try to apply medicine before we've received an accurate diagnosis of the problem, we may do more harm than good if we're using the wrong medicine. At best, we will merely alleviate the symptoms—but the underlying cause is what we need to address.

A spiritual diagnosis, therefore, is recognizing and identifying the source of the difficulty by its signs and symptoms; investigating and analyzing its cause or nature; and making a statement or conclusion based on this observation and analysis. Each of these steps can be achieved only by relying on the guidance of the Holy Spirit, the true Diagnostician of all our problems.

EVERY PROBLEM HAS A SPIRITUAL ROOT— AND A SPIRITUAL SOLUTION

The Bible tells us the ultimate source of all trials and difficulties. Every human problem—whether it is spiritual, physical, mental, emotional, or psychological—has a spiritual root. All evil stems from the fall of humankind, when Adam and Eve committed the original sin in the Garden of Eden by rebelling against God.

Conversely, all human problems have spiritual solutions. The diagnoses of our adversities will always reflect this spiritual root. If we look to secular solutions alone to solve spiritual problems, we will be applying the wrong medicine, because secular solutions are incomplete cures. This is not to say we won't ever receive wisdom or good advice from non-spiritual sources. And some solutions to our difficulties involve plain common sense. But we need to remember that all wisdom ultimately comes from God and that He is the One we are to look to for guidance and help.

LOOK TO GOD FOR GUIDANCE AND HELP.

Again, the spiritual root of our traumas is the fall of humankind. The presence of sin in the earth is the source of every problem that confronts us. Because sin entered the world, we now face various trials. Some of the causes of these trials are...

➤ *the temptations of the world* (See Matthew 13:22; 1 Timothy 6:9–10.)

➤ *the lusts of our own carnal nature* [walking according to our sinful nature instead of walking according to the Spirit] (See Romans 8:1, 5–8; James 1:13–15.)

➤ *the wiles of the devil* (See Ephesians 6:11; 1 Peter 5:8.)

> ➤ *the persecution that believers of the Lord Jesus Christ undergo as His followers* (See Matthew 5:10–12; John 15:20; 2 Timothy 3:12.)
> ➤ *the temporary removal of God's hedge of protection for His glory and our greater good* (See Job 1:6–12; 2:1–6; 42:1–17.)

As we learned earlier, there are times, as in the case of Job, when God will remove the hedge of protection around us for a season, and we will experience various trials. These trials are not punishments; rather, God allows them in order to carry out His purposes and to bring glory to His name.

SOME REASONS FOR OUR TRIALS ARE A MYSTERY

It is very important for us to recognize that we may never identify the cause of every problem we face, in the sense that we can fully answer the question as to "why" certain things happen to us. Some of the reasons for our trials and suffering will remain a mystery until we go to be with the Lord. However, what we can usually identify is the particular area or areas—the world, the flesh, the devil, persecution for the sake of Christ, the furtherance of God's glory—to which our trials are most closely connected. Then we can respond to these trials in a way that will bring us the most spiritual benefit, healing, and growth.

THE DANGERS OF "SELF-DIAGNOSIS"

We have all had the experience of attempting to diagnose our illnesses based only on our symptoms and limited knowledge. However, this type of guesswork can be dangerous. I taught school for a number of years before going into full-time ministry. I remember a student of mine named David who was very quiet and introverted. This behavior, in itself, was not cause for alarm, but David was also pale and lethargic and seemed to lack the certain "spark" that I had noticed in my other third-grade students. When I mentioned my observations to his parents, they both dismissed my concern by saying, "Oh, he's always been like that. Maybe we should just increase his vitamin intake or make sure he gets to bed an hour earlier."

I continued to press the issue, until David's parents finally took him for a full battery of tests. The test results showed that he had a very serious case of juvenile diabetes that, if left unchecked, could greatly impair his development or even threaten his life. David was then put on a corrective diet and given the proper medication, and his condition immediately improved. Yet if his parents had continued to guess about the reasons for his symptoms, and the proper diagnosis had not been made, the outcome might have been deadly.

It is crucial that we do not try to guess about or "self-diagnose" the reasons for our trials, so that we won't jump to incorrect conclusions or fall into presumption. Doctors encourage us to do regular *self-examinations* under their guidance to check for certain potential problems. However, only a doctor, who is a medical expert, can make a proper diagnosis. *Self-diagnosis* can be a dangerous practice if we undertake it without knowledge, practice, and skill. As we will discover later in this chapter, the way we protect ourselves against presumption is by going to God in prayer; by seeking the counsel of a trusted pastor, counselor, or friend; and by reading and studying the Word of God. Often, the process of diagnosing our trials requires us to wait on God to answer in His own time and way. In these instances, we are to hold onto God in faith, trusting in His love and purposes.

It is important first to evaluate the causes of our problems and to identify them. Later chapters in this book present in greater detail how to treat our trials with the appropriate spiritual medicine.

THE WAITING ROOM

The emergency room is the busiest place in a hospital. Although the people who fill the waiting area are there for various reasons, they all have the same vacant look on their faces. Their loved ones are tucked away in cubicles somewhere. They are left to struggle to remain calm as they wait for the doctors to give them their diagnoses.

Whether you are in an "emergency room cubicle" waiting for the remedy of *your* life struggle or in the "waiting room" listening for an update on *someone else's* condition, you must avoid the temptation to make your own diagnosis and devise your own remedy for the situation.

When you ask God to help you in your adversity, you may not receive the answer you expect. That is when you will be tempted to devise your own answer. The most difficult thing to do in a waiting room is to *wait*. During that period of waiting, fear and intimidation can wreak havoc on the mind and the emotions.

TRYING TO FIGURE IT OUT

At times of emotional stress during my illness, like most people I felt tempted to ask God why I had to go through such a terrible time of testing. However, I knew that God was in control. When we face a crisis, it is easy for us to question God's goodness. God told Job, however, that He owes no one an explanation for His actions because everything belongs to Him. (See Job 41:11.) He is sovereign. We often look for answers, but sometimes we just won't receive the answers to our questions in this life. God withholds the answers for His own reasons. Faith requires that we live as we should, trusting God, despite our unanswered questions. We can count on His love and grace.

WHEN FACING A CRISIS, IT'S EASY TO QUESTION GOD.

It is normal for us as human beings to look at difficult circumstances we are experiencing and to try to figure out the whys and wherefores of their existence in our lives. You will discover that often well-meaning friends will jump to conclusions and feel that they have the correct explanation for your situation when, like Job's friends, they don't have the complete picture. I am annoyed when well-meaning believers in the church come to me with weak explanations and their own brand of reasoning for why I am experiencing certain difficulties and situations in my life. At these times, I am always reminded that God knows my situation and loves me. Therefore, I continue to trust Him, even though I may not understand why my life is going the way that it is at a given time.

MISCONCEPTIONS ABOUT SUFFERING

The book of Job is a theological treatise about suffering and divine sovereignty. It is also a gripping drama of riches to rags to riches, and a striking picture of faith that endures. Job encountered so much suffering and devastation in his life that many of us shudder at the very thought of ever having to experience what he had to go through. Job experienced extreme physical pain, as well as grief over the loss of his children and possessions. His grief placed him at the crossroads of his faith.

Throughout the book of Job, Job's friends Eliphaz, Bildad, and Zophar—who had originally come to comfort him—gave their own reasons for Job's sufferings. They advised him to admit his sin and ask God for forgiveness. Overwhelmed by suffering, Job was not comforted but condemned by his friends. Each of their views represents a well-known way of understanding suffering.

GOD USED JOB'S SUFFERING TO SHATTER MISCONCEPTIONS.

Eliphaz the Temanite said Job was suffering because he had sinned. Bildad the Shuhite said Job wouldn't admit that he had sinned, and that was why he was suffering. Zophar the Naamathite said Job's sin deserved even more suffering than he had experienced. Then a fourth man who had come to be with Job in his suffering, Elihu the Buzite, said that God was using suffering for the purpose of molding and training Job.

God eventually proved that each of these explanations had less than the whole answer. God used Job's experience to shatter many misconceptions about Himself and His ways. Some of these misconceptions are:

➤ God *always* rewards godliness with riches.
➤ God *always* protects us and our loved ones from harm.
➤ Sickness and calamity are *always* a sign of God's displeasure.

The problem with the above misconceptions is attaching the word *always* to them. Applying the word *always* to our situations or the situations of others can cause us to automatically assume we know the reasons, explanations, and answers to all problems.

It is true that, in some cases, God has given wealth to bless those who believe in Him. Job himself was given great material wealth both before and after his suffering. On the other hand, many of God's people have not had great material wealth. (See, for example, the widow of Zarephath in 1 Kings 17.) There are times when God *does* miraculously protect us from harm, and there are times when God allows His hedge of protection to be removed from our lives for His purposes. (See those who were rescued and those who died for their faith in Hebrews 11.) Sometimes God has allowed people to experience sickness as a result of His displeasure. (See, for example, the disciplining of Miriam in Numbers 12.) At other times, God makes it clear that some people suffer illnesses not through any fault of their own, but to fulfill His greater purposes. (See, for example, the account in John 9 of the man born blind.)

You have to be careful when well-meaning friends come to you ready to make a quick assessment about your situation, figuring that certain things happened for this reason and that reason. I almost fell into guilt because some things happened in my life—like divorce—for which I couldn't find any reason. Reasons give us a degree of security. If I could have pointed to something that I had done—some decision or some choice I had made—that had caused certain things to happen, I would have felt better. Yet it can be dangerous when people say, "Well, this happened because you didn't do that right" or, "If you had done this, that wouldn't have happened to you." We have to be careful about allowing other people to tell us the reason for our adversities. That's what Job's friends did, and all of them were *wrong.*

TWO CHOICES

At his deepest point of despair, Job was driven back to the basics of his faith in God. He had only two choices: he could curse God and die, as his wife recommended (Job 2:9);

or he could trust God and draw strength from Him to continue on (Job 27:2–6). Job always kept his integrity and never cursed God. However, in his grief, he wanted to give up—to die and be freed from his suffering (Job 3:11–24). But God did not grant Job's request. He had a greater plan for him. Like Job, our tendency is to want to give up and get out when the going gets tough. To trust God in the good times is commendable, but to trust Him during the difficult times tests us to our limits. Even when we cannot figure out why certain things are happening to

> **WE TEND TO WANT TO GIVE UP WHEN THE GOING GETS TOUGH.**

us, we should trust that God is in control, whether our struggles are large or small. Proverbs 3:5–6 says, *"Trust in the LORD with all your heart, and lean not on your own understanding; in all your ways acknowledge Him, and He shall direct your paths."* (See also Proverbs 29:25; 30:5; Psalm 56:3; 91:2; 115:11; 125:1.)

WHAT'S GOING ON?

As I said earlier, being informed about the reasons for our trials brings us a sense of security. It is natural to want to know what is happening in our lives. Job wanted to know what was going on, why he was suffering, why he was experiencing such devastation in his life. As we read the book of Job, we can sense his frustration. Elihu claimed to have the answer to Job's biggest question, "Why doesn't God tell me what is happening?"

Elihu told Job that God was trying to answer him, but that he was not listening. Elihu misjudged God on this point. If God were to answer all our questions, we would have no need to continue to rely on Him. Remember that God does not allow testing for His benefit, but for ours. What if God had warned Job by saying, "Job, satan is going to test you and afflict you, but in the end you will be healed and get everything back"? Would his trust and faith in God's sovereignty have been strengthened? Job's greatest test was not his pain and suffering, but that he did not know *why* these things were happening to him. Our greatest test may be that we must trust God's goodness and rely on Him even when we don't understand why our lives are going in a certain way. We must learn to trust God, who is good, and not in the goodness of life.

WHY DO BAD THINGS HAPPEN TO GOD'S PEOPLE?

In my book *Don't Die in the Winter...Your Season Is Coming,* I point out that there have been seasons and times in my life when it seemed as if everything negative that *could* happen *did* happen, and happened all at once. These times were very stressful and tearful for me. Yet in our spiritual lives, there are always seasons of pain and seasons of gain. In order for us to gain a deeper anointing and commitment for what God has called us to do, we must have seasons of change. I have found that God does His greatest work in the desert places of our lives. Endurance plays a major role in our victory in Christ.

The word *endurance* does not conjure up warm, wonderful feelings for me. It signifies affliction, withstanding hardship, and holding steady against prolonged pain and distress. God has taken me through painful circumstances so that I might understand the suffering of others and touch them in His name. He has led me through desert places so that I will have compassion in my heart for those who are weary. *"The Sovereign LORD has given me an instructed tongue, to know the word that sustains the weary"* (Isaiah 50:4).

Every one of us, at one time or another, will experience suffering in this life. Often, the suffering will be so great and difficult that it will upset the equilibrium of our lives—to the extent that we will never be the same again. At such times, many Christians ask, "Why do bad things happen to good people?"

Job was a *good man,* but he experienced *bad things.* Job was a prosperous farmer living in the land of Uz. He had thousands of sheep, camels, and other livestock. He had a large family and many servants to take care of his every need. He was a blessed man.

Job 1:1 calls Job *"blameless and upright."* He was a good man because he *"feared God and shunned evil"* (v. 1). He respected, worshipped, and obeyed God. He did everything he could to do good, avoid evil, and keep from sinning.

Job was a *good man.*

But sometimes, bad things happen to good people.

THE ACCUSER OF THE BRETHREN

The reason for Job's trials, as we saw in chapter one, was that God had removed His hedge of protection from Job's life for a season, so that His glory and power over satan could be revealed in a striking and definitive way. It surprises some people to hear that satan indeed has access to God. Yet the reason he is called the *"accuser of* [the] *brethren"* (Revelation 12:10) and the adversary is that he often goes into the presence of God to make accusations against believers. He actively looks for people to attack with temptation. He looks for people who have let their prayer guard down. He looks for people

ANYONE COMMITTED TO GOD CAN EXPECT SATAN'S ATTACKS.

who are saved but weak in their commitment. He looks for people who don't stand on the Word of God, because they don't *know* the Word of God. He looks for people who are lukewarm, who seldom apply the Word to their lives, and who are straddling the fence between the church and the world. He looks for these people so that he can devour them. *"Be sober, be vigilant; because your adversary the devil walks about like a roaring lion, seeking whom he may devour"* (1 Peter 5:8). The devil spends his days and nights actively looking for someone to attack.

Any person who is committed to God can expect satan's attacks. Satan is God's enemy. He hates God, and he hates God's people. Satan knows that he cannot steal our salvation because Christ's work on the cross is a finished work, and our redemption is sealed and safe. The Word of God says that nothing and no one—not even satan—can snatch us out of the Father's hand (John 10:29), so our salvation is secure.

Satan *does* try to hinder God's work in believers by weakening their faith in Him and by limiting their prayer lives, their strength, and their commitment. It is important to remember, however, that satan himself is limited by God's power. He can do only what God permits him to do. Job was a model of trust and obedience. God knew Job's character and how he would react to his sufferings. Therefore, He permitted satan to attack him in an extremely harsh manner.

God deeply loves us, but this truth is not a guarantee that our faith, trust, and obedience will shelter us from adversity. Some of the worst things happen to some of the best people. Setbacks, tragedies, chaos, and crises—all of these problems strike the saved as well as the unsaved. Evil exists in this world. Good and evil are opposing forces that constantly contend for the heart of humankind and will continue to do so until Jesus comes to set matters straight.

So satan attacked Job, and Job lost all of his ten children and his many possessions. Then the devil caused great sickness and physical suffering to come upon him. *Sometimes bad things happen to good people.*

VIEWS OF SUFFERING

Job was called a good man because he feared God. He respected, worshipped, and obeyed Him. He was also good because he stayed away from evil. He did not allow sin to creep into his life or temptation to overcome him. Yet if Job was really a good man, his three friends would have had to drop their theory that suffering is always God's punishment for evil actions. However, instead of considering that there might be another viewpoint, they cut off the discussion. They were convinced that Job had some *hidden* fault or sin. They felt there was no point in talking to Job if he would not confess his sin. But Job knew that he had lived uprightly before God and man and had avoided wrong thoughts and actions. He wasn't about to invent a sin just to satisfy his friends.

There are four basic views of suffering:

➢ *Satan's view:* People will believe in God only when they are prospering and not suffering. (This view is false.)

➤ *The view of Job's three friends:* Suffering is God's judgment for sin. (This is not always true.)

➤ *Elihu's view:* God uses suffering to teach, discipline, and refine. (This is true, but is an incomplete explanation.)

➤ *God's view:* Suffering causes us to trust God for who He is, not just for what He does and what He gives us.

Job's question about why believers experience troubles and suffering is timeless. Even after a long debate, Job's wise friends were unable to answer that question, just as people today are unable to answer it. Job's friends made a serious error of presumption, for which God rebuked them. They assumed that trouble comes only when people commit sin. We see the same error today in those who assert that sickness and lack of material blessing are signs of unconfessed sin and a lack of faith—period.

The truth is that no one is truly good except God (Matthew 19:17). On a relative scale, some people are "better" than others. They may have higher morals or show more love for others. Yet in our fallen world, bad things happen to "good" and "bad" people alike. Both believers and unbelievers experience the tragic consequences of sin. God is permitting evil to exist in the world for a time. We may have **GOD KNOWS WHAT HE IS DOING.** no answers as to why God allows evil, but we can be confident in the knowledge that He is all-powerful and knows what He is doing.

Job agonized over his situation. His wife slandered him, his friends accused him, but all his troubles drew him closer to God than ever before. The next time you face trials and dilemmas, look to God for strength. Only then will you find that God is waiting to show His love and compassion to you. If you can trust Him regardless of your situation, you will win the victory and eliminate one of satan's greatest footholds in your life. If God is your foundation, you can never lose everything.

HELPFUL AND HARMFUL REACTIONS TO SUFFERING

Suffering is helpful when:

➢ we turn to God for understanding, endurance, and deliverance.

➢ we ask important questions that we might not take the time to ask or think about during our normal routines.

➢ we are prepared by it to identify with and comfort others who suffer.

➢ we become open to being helped by others who are obeying God.

➢ we are ready to learn from a trustworthy God.

➢ we realize we can identify with what Christ suffered on the cross for us.

➢ we are sensitized to the amount of suffering in the world.

Suffering is harmful when:

➢ we become hardened and reject God.

➢ we refuse to ask any questions and miss lessons that might be good for us.

➢ we allow it to make us self-centered and selfish.

➢ we withdraw from the help others can give.

➢ we reject the fact that God can bring good out of calamity.

➢ we accuse God of being unjust and perhaps lead others to reject Him.

➢ we refuse to be open to any changes in our lives.

Because of his hatred for God, satan will do whatever he can to discourage you and cause you to give up and turn your back on God. Don't allow your suffering to make you bitter toward the only One who can deliver you. God is beyond our comprehension, and we cannot always know why He allows each instance of suffering to come into our lives. Our part is simply to remain faithful. God is in control of the world, and only He understands why the good are allowed to suffer. This will become clear to us only as we see God for who He is. We must courageously accept what God allows to happen in our lives and remain firmly committed to Him.

PERSECUTION AS A SOURCE OF TRIAL

Satan's attacks against us take many forms. However, persecution for the sake of Christ is a particular form of trial. God allows persecution so that He may train us in Christian maturity.

The Bible tells us in many passages of Scripture that if we love God, we will experience persecution and suffering. (See, for example John 15:18–19; 2 Timothy 3:12.) The first century church grew from a handful of committed followers of Jesus Christ to a dynamic, growing community of believers. Yet as the church grew, so did the persecution and suffering of God's people. These adversities caused the church to go underground. Many believers fled their homes and moved to other towns or regions for fear of their lives. But they took their faith with them, and as a result, the church grew. Satan had a plan of destruction; but God had a bigger plan: persecution would be a catalyst for the spread of Christianity and the explosive growth of the church.

SUFFERING IS THE TRAINING GROUND FOR CHRISTIAN MATURITY.

Again, suffering is often the training ground for Christian maturity. To train means "to prepare, to prime, to teach, or to discipline." When we talk about coming to maturity in Christ, invariably we are talking about a process that includes suffering. This process may not always be comforting, but its purpose and design come from the heart of God.

LONGING FOR THE OLD FAMILIAR WAYS

The book of Hebrews is a masterful document written to Christians who were struggling with their newfound faith. These were mainly second-generation Jewish Christians, some of whom were considering a return to Judaism, with its laws, customs, rituals, and sacrifices. The new Christian doctrine was being scrutinized. To these Hebrews, Christianity seemed vague and ambiguous. The emphasis wasn't so much on doing works and obeying specific laws, but on loving God with all your heart, mind, soul, and strength, and loving your neighbor as yourself (Mark 12:30–31). They found it somewhat difficult to understand that if you confessed with your mouth that Jesus is Lord and believed in your heart that God raised Jesus from the dead, you would be saved (Romans 10:9). The "law of love" in Christ—which encompasses all the Old Testament commandments (Romans 13:8)—was not fully understood by them.

These Christians knew that living a sinless life under the Old Testament law was impossible and oppressive. However, the old system was appealing to them because it was familiar and could give them a degree of comfort—it gave a person set things to do rather than having to live by this law of love. In their insecurity and immaturity, these new Christians were considering a return to the old familiar ways. Before Jesus had ascended to the right hand of His Father, He had said He would come back and take them to be with Him. It had been over thirty years, and He had not yet returned. Many new Christians were becoming discouraged and disheartened. Now that the original excitement of Pentecost had worn off and the dust had settled, many people had gone back to business as usual.

THE STRESS OF PERSECUTION

But in addition to the confusion and questions—and perhaps the real source of their longing for the old ways—they were beginning to suffer much persecution. Sometimes they had to conceal their faith, and pray and worship in secret. Sometimes they had to flee to other towns for safety. I can imagine them thinking, "It wasn't supposed to be like this. We are the light of the world. We are the salt of the earth. We are the living stones, the royal priesthood, the holy nation, the chosen generation; but we're hurting, struggling, suffering, agonizing. This wasn't what we had anticipated."

How many of us have struggled with similar feelings? Perhaps some of the excitement of your newfound faith and church home have worn off. It's not as much fun as it was at first, because now you are being called into accountability and responsibility.

Some of us are uncomfortable with this reality. When the pressures of responsibility and persecution come against us, the old life in the world starts to look good again. People in the world don't have to tithe, study the Bible, turn the other cheek, or live a holy life. Unbelievers don't seem to suffer persecution or be confronted with the same kind of hardships and opposition we encounter. We, like the Hebrews, are hurting, struggling, suffering, agonizing.

PERSECUTION FROM FELLOW BELIEVERS

Perhaps the hardest thing to take is when persecution comes from fellow believers or those who claim to be believers. When Paul was imprisoned for preaching the Gospel, other preachers, who were supposed to be his co-laborers in the Gospel, used his suffering to further their own ministries. They were envious of Paul's apostolic power and authority, as well as his success and immense giftedness in ministry, and so they attempted to damage his reputation.

I want you to know, brethren, that the things which happened to me have actually turned out for the furtherance of the gospel, so that it has become evident to the whole palace guard, and to all the rest, that my chains are in Christ; and most of the brethren in the Lord, having become confident by my chains, are much more bold to speak the word without fear. Some indeed preach Christ even from envy and strife, and some also from good will: the former preach Christ from selfish ambition, not sincerely, supposing to add affliction to my chains; but the latter out of love, knowing that I am appointed for the defense of the gospel. What then? Only that in every way, whether in pretense or in truth, Christ is preached; and in this I rejoice, yes, and will rejoice.

(Philippians 1:12–18)

Paul was well-known as an apostle and received much attention from believers. Other preachers were jealous of him, and therefore did not like him. They probably gossiped about him, preached sermons against him, and attacked his good name and reputation by saying that God was punishing him because of some secret sin in his life. They said that Paul's imprisonment was God's way of chastening him and correcting him. Paul's experience teaches us that, even when we are living right, not everybody will be happy about the fact that we are being blessed and mightily used by God.

NOT EVERYONE WILL BE HAPPY IF YOU ARE BEING USED BY GOD.

I often warn other ministers that sometimes those who work with you and beside you will be your greatest detractors and reputation destroyers. They will make up all kinds of stories, even drag your name through the mud, hoping that the larger churches will stop calling you and the big conferences will no longer book you, because the scandal will tarnish your good name. Then maybe there will be an open space for them.

You need to know that you will never promote yourself by tearing somebody else down. My grandmother used to say that if you try to dig a grave for somebody by destroying his or her reputation, you had better dig two graves—one for the person you are trying to destroy and one for yourself! You can never harm anyone else without harming yourself, too.

BLESSING THROUGH PERSECUTION

Paul's perspective was that these people were not harming him, but rather helping him. He said, in essence, "Their lying about me and dragging my name through the mud is like free advertisement for the Gospel; it is like putting my message on the six o'clock news or running a feature story in the local newspaper." Paul told the Philippians that his imprisonment was not a hindrance to him, but that being in jail gave him a whole new set of opportunities to witness and a whole new group of people to preach to. "Let them slander me; my purpose is to preach. After a while, everybody's going to know me and the Good News I have to share." (See Philippians 1:12–18.)

Paul's many sufferings (see Galatians 6:17) had shown him that unforeseen blessings can come out of our adversities. When we make God our priority, He will cause all things to work out for our good. *"And we know that all things work together for good to those who love God, to those who are the called according to His purpose"* (Romans 8:28).

GOD DISCIPLINES THOSE HE LOVES

Again, suffering is the training ground for Christian maturity, whether it is for our general growth in faith or for correction when we turn away from God. It is one of God's ways of disciplining us. Hebrews 12:5 says, *"Do not despise the chastening of the LORD, nor be discouraged when you are rebuked by Him; for whom the LORD loves He chastens, and scourges every son whom He receives."* Don't take the discipline of the Lord lightly, and don't lose heart when you are chastised by Him, for the Lord disciplines those whom He loves.

CORRECTION IS A SIGN OF LOVE

Hebrews 12:7 says, *"If you endure chastening, God deals with you as with sons; for what son is there whom a father does not chasten?"* We need to endure suffering for the sake of discipline, for God is treating us as His children. Who loves his child more—the parent who allows his child to do what will harm him, or the one who corrects, trains, and even punishes his child to help him learn what is right? It is never pleasant to be corrected and disciplined by God,

GOD'S DISCIPLINE IS A SIGN OF HIS LOVE FOR US.

but His discipline is a sign of His deep love for us. When God corrects you, see it as proof of His love, and ask Him what He is trying to teach you.

Sometimes, when I discipline my children, they react by saying, "Mom, you are so mean!" Does that sound familiar to you? When my children respond in that way, I tell them that

I'm disciplining them because I love them, and because it is my responsibility to instruct and correct them. Correction is a proof of love. Correction is discipline, but a little child sees it only as suffering. When God corrects you, He does so because He loves you and wants Christ to live in you. In His sovereign knowledge, He knows that the struggle you are facing is the best way for you to grow and mature in Him.

It is so important to remember that God never *causes* sickness, problems, destruction, or death for the purpose of disciplining us. That is not scriptural. However, God does *use* sickness, problems, destruction, and even death to bring about His will in the lives of those He loves.

Jesus did not cause Lazarus's death, but He used his death to work a miracle before the people and to bring glory to God, who is the Giver of life.

God did not cause Hezekiah's sickness or the suffering it brought, but He used his sickness to build his faith, to cause him to pray, and bring glory to God, the Healer of life.

God did not cause the persecution in Paul's life or the suffering it brought, but He used Paul's thorn in the flesh to bring glory to Himself, the Power of life. That is why God said to Paul, *"My grace is sufficient for you, for My strength is made perfect in weakness"* (2 Corinthians 12:9). Paul learned to glory in his sufferings so that the power of Christ could rest on him (v. 9).

GOD KNOWS OUR HEARTS

Sometimes we experience trials as a result of our stubborn, willful disobedience to God. All of us as children of God want to love Him and please Him, but many of us want to hear the bottom line first. We don't want to volunteer for anything that is going to be difficult or painful. But remember that Hebrews 12:8 says that if we do not experience the discipline that all children are given, then we are illegitimate and not really sons and daughters of God.

Proverbs 15:32 says, *"He who disdains instruction despises his own soul, but he who heeds rebuke gets understanding."* Our fleshly nature never likes to be corrected. We never like to be told we are wrong. But we don't know our own hearts. *"The heart is deceitful above all things, and desperately wicked; who can know it?"* (Jeremiah 17:9). God is the only One who really knows our hearts and motives. *"I, the LORD, search the heart, I test the mind, even to give every man according to his ways, according to the fruit of his doings"* (v. 10).

God goes after our character flaws, and when we truly love God, we want those flaws dealt with and removed so that we can grow to maturity and full stature in Christ (Ephesians 4:13).

God has set in motion the "law of sowing and reaping." (See Galatians 6:7.) When we as His children go our own way and do our own thing, sometimes God will step back, take away His protection for a season, and allow us to reap what we have sown. However, He does this out of love and a desire to correct us. We can actually be comforted when this happens, because it is proof that we belong to Him. Remember that He disciplines those whom He loves (Hebrews 12:6).

Even those who are saved can be carnal and *"walk according to the flesh"* (Romans 8:1). When we do this, we're not being disciples, not being true followers of Jesus. We have one foot in the world and one in the church. Paul wrote to the Corinthians and the Ephesians that they were spiritually immature. They had not allowed the Spirit of God to take full control of their lives. Paul said that there are two kinds of people: those

> EVEN THOSE WHO ARE SAVED CAN BE CARNALLY MINDED.

who allow themselves to be controlled by the Holy Spirit and those who allow themselves to be controlled by their lower nature. He said that there is no middle ground, no gray area, and no straddling the fence when it comes to being yielded to the Spirit. When we walk *"according to the Spirit"* (Romans 8:1), we are truly led of the Lord and have the power to no longer obey the old evil nature within us.

CHRISTIAN MATURITY IS NOT AUTOMATIC

When we are saved, we sometimes think that we are automatically going to experience spiritual maturity. However, living the Christian life and becoming a mature follower of Christ is a process that takes time, commitment, responsibility, and accountability if we are to grow. Although we receive a new nature when we become Christians, we don't automatically have all good thoughts, attitudes, and actions.

The Bible says we are to leave the old nature behind. It is spiritually unhealthy for you to live according to the flesh. When you live according to your old nature, you allow harmful things into your life that will choke your spirit. It is the equivalent to endangering your body by breathing in toxic fumes, cutting off the flow of healthy oxygen and making it impossible for you to breathe. God wants you to be a mature believer; therefore, you need to breathe in the refreshing air of the Holy Spirit and allow it to fill your life.

When we don't realize the serious consequences of living according to the flesh, then we resist yielding to the Holy Spirit and His control, and we end up being carnal. (See Romans 8:5–6.) This doesn't mean that we're no longer Christians, but it does mean that we're living in an unnatural way for a Christian, and this will cause us many problems.

Even if a person has been a Christian for many years, his or her faith may still be immature. The apostle Paul said that to focus our minds on sin and carnal things is *"death,"* but to focus our minds on spiritual things is *"life and peace"* (v. 6). Paul used a very strong term in speaking of sin. He said that sin and carnal things bring **death**.

WHAT IS YOUR CONDITION?

Sin always brings corruption, death, and decay to everything that it touches. Christians cannot be spiritually dead, as unbelievers are. However, when you as a believer lack commitment, are not sold out to the things of God, and are not learning to be the follower of Christ that God has called you to be, you might not be dead, but in terms of your spiritual health, you can be in one of the following conditions: "fair" condition, "serious" condition, "critical" condition, or "life support."

Fair Condition: Christians in fair condition may still be on the right track overall, but they are straddling the fence between Christ and the world. They are like a patient whose broken leg has healed but needs to be strengthened and exercised so that the person can walk and eventually run again. They may know the Word of God and desire to live according to the Spirit, but they are still weak in certain areas because they yield so easily to temptation.

Serious Condition: Some Christians have gone beyond fair condition; they are in serious condition, like a patient in need of a blood transfusion. People who are in serious condition have a difficult time growing in God because they allow the spirit of guilt—guilt for how they used to live and what they used to be like—to affect their service for God now. They are stuck in the past. They keep reliving the mistakes and wrong choices they have made. Somewhere along the way, they have forgotten that the blood of Jesus Christ covers their sin and past transgressions.

Critical Condition: There are certain Christians who are in critical condition, like a patient in desperate need of a heart transplant. They require a total change of heart, mind, and attitude, so that they will realize they are not to be conformed to this world, but transformed by the renewing of their minds (Romans 12:2). God will use adversity to change our hearts and minds so that we can think right, love right, and do right.

Life Support: Other Christians are in need of full life support, like a patient who hangs in the balance between life and death. To be in need of spiritual life support is a grave condition. At times, it's hard to tell if such people are spiritually dead or alive. They never exercise their spiritual muscles, so their Christian lives begin to atrophy and deteriorate. Sometimes trials are needed in order to wake believers up to the fact that they need to become spiritually alive again.

RESPONDING TO GOD'S DISCIPLINE

So God uses suffering as a training ground for Christian maturity. He also uses it to revive the declining spiritual life of His people. When you feel as if you are losing heart during such trials, take courage. When God corrects you, see it as proof of His love and ask Him what He is trying to teach you.

We can respond to discipline in several ways:

➢ We can accept it with empty resignation.

➢ We can accept it with self-pity, thinking we don't deserve it.

➢ We can be angry and resent God for it.

OR

➢ We can accept it gratefully as the appropriate discipline of our loving, heavenly Father.

No matter what storms, difficulties, problems, burdens, or pain you suffer, you can be a happy, victorious, confident, overcoming believer. When you are living and walking in the Spirit, relying on Him, yielded to Him, and fully obedient to Him, you can be assured that

GOD'S WAYS ARE ALWAYS...
good,
perfect,
true,
right,
just,
best.

Like Paul, you will discover that unforeseen blessings can come out of your adversities, and that when you put God's interests first, He will use all things for your good (Romans 8:28).

MAKING THE RIGHT DIAGNOSIS

We have looked at various reasons for adversity in the lives of believers. When assessing our trials, we need to exercise patience, because understanding our trials is not an exact science; it will probably take time and perseverance.

In order for the doctors to be sure of their diagnosis of my illness, I had to undergo a variety of tests because my symptoms could have been caused by something other than spinal meningitis; every disease has its own specific signs and symptoms. In addition, each patient requires a specialized treatment that meets the medical needs of that individual. We must keep in mind that God's *strong medicine* is specific to the particular personalities and needs of His people. One person may undergo a trial for one reason, while another person may undergo a very similar trial for a completely different reason. Moreover, we may never fully understand the reasons we undergo certain trials. It is important that we do not jump to conclusions about our adversities.

DON'T JUMP TO CONCLUSIONS ABOUT YOUR ADVERSITY.

Since the symptoms of adversity can look alike when their causes are really different, how do we accurately diagnose our spiritual troubles so that we will be able to apply the appropriate spiritual medicine?

The best doctors use a combination of knowledge, wisdom, and experience. A doctor makes a diagnosis based on the following measures:

➤ Medical knowledge

➤ Observation of the patient's symptoms

➤ Testing

To determine the true source of your difficulty, you need to draw on *spiritual* knowledge, observation of your circumstances, and testing. These measures are best determined through prayer, wise counsel, and the test of God's Word.

PRAYER

Prayer is your greatest source of hearing from God about your adversity because God is all-knowing. As a physician uses medical knowledge, we can go to God as the Source of all spiritual knowledge. Yield to the Lordship of Christ and the working of the Spirit in your life, and then ask God to show you what He wants you to learn through your situation. The key to prayer is to have an open mind and an open ear to the Lord so that you can hear what God wants to reveal to you.

I know it sounds easy to say, "Just go to God in prayer and let Him speak to you about what the real problem is."

However, when you are not attuned to the voice of God because you do not pray sincerely and consistently, you can sometimes tell yourself things you want to hear, and then make yourself believe that you're hearing from Him. Remember, satan is a great imitator and can mimic the voice of God. He may try to suggest things to you to make you feel condemned or to get you off track. At other times, you may find yourself in a state of denial, where you don't want to hear certain things from God. It is imperative that you practice hearing God's voice by having regular times of prayer, so that when adversity comes, you will be able to recognize His voice as you go to Him for wisdom and guidance. A mother is able to distinguish her own baby's cry from the cries of hundreds of other babies. Similarly, you should be so accustomed to hearing God speak to you through prayer and the study of His Word that you will recognize His voice in the midst of the noise of your own thoughts, others' opinions, and satan's attempts at deception. (See John 10:27.)

TRUSTED COUNSELOR OR FRIEND

Whether or not you are experienced in hearing the voice of God, talking to a trusted pastor, counselor, or friend who is spiritually mature and strong in the things of God is a good practice when you are going through a trial. This is the equivalent of a medical doctor's "observation." Sometimes it's hard for us to make an objective evaluation of ourselves because our emotions can interfere with our ability to hear from God. A person who is spiritually mature can help us to determine what is truly going on in our lives.

> **TALK TO SOMEONE WHO IS SPIRITUALLY MATURE.**

Keep in mind that a trusted counselor or friend is not someone who heaps guilt on you under the pretext of offering godly counsel. The person you go to for help should be someone you trust to be honest and to give you advice based on the Word of God.

GOD'S WORD

Just as doctors run medical tests, we need to test everything by the Word of God. To effectively do this, you must be reading and studying the Word on a continual basis. When you are constantly studying God's Word, it is going to help you to see the truth more clearly. In this way, you will be better able to compare what you are thinking and the advice you are receiving with what the Bible says. Then you can assess whether or not your thoughts and the counsel of others line up with the Word of God.

Again, a doctor uses X rays because they give a deeper look into the internal structure and workings of the body. The Word of God acts in the same way. When you study the Bible, it is like looking at an X ray of your inner self. Some of us might not always want to see ourselves as fully as God sees us. However, when we do, and when we ask for His help in changing us so that we may become like Christ, the Word will give us the proper diagnosis for any situation. Then the right spiritual medicine can be applied for our healing.

Pray to God, talk to mature Christians, and read and study God's Word to determine the source of your adversity. Then you will be ready for God's *strong medicine* that is designed to meet your every need.

Pray this prayer as you seek God about the reason for your trial:

> *Lord, I ask for Your knowledge and understanding about the trial that I am currently going through. Help me to know the source of my adversity so that I may know the proper "spiritual medicine" to take. Teach me what You want me to learn. Help me to be patient and persevering in the midst of the stress and uncertainty, and keep me from blaming You for my adversity. Give me grace to accept my circumstances, especially if it is not for me to know the full reasons for my suffering. I pray these things in the name of Jesus, who was "a man of sorrows and acquainted with grief" and who is also my Great Physician. Amen.*

 SPIRITUAL VITAMINS

☐ Think of specific ways in which God has helped you in past times of trouble. Write down one of these examples in the form of a faith testimony on a sheet of paper and refer to it often this week. Read Hebrews 11 to strengthen your faith.

☐ For the next week, pray the prayer at the end of chapter three, so that you will have an open mind and heart to hear what God is saying to you about your adversity.

☐ Read and memorize these verses so you may remember that every problem has a spiritual root—and a spiritual solution:

> *For all that is in the world; the lust of the flesh, the lust of the eyes, and the pride of life; is not of the Father but is of the world.* (1 John 2:16)

> *Search me, O God, and know my heart; try me, and know my anxieties; and see if there is any wicked way in me, and lead me in the way everlasting.* (Psalm 139:23–24)

> *Be sober, be vigilant; because your adversary the devil walks about like a roaring lion, seeking whom he may devour.* (1 Peter 5:8)

> *For the word of God is living and powerful, and sharper than any two-edged sword, piercing even to the division of soul and spirit, and of joints and marrow, and is a discerner of the thoughts and intents of the heart.* (Hebrews 4:12)

4

PAINKILLERS
Numbing the Pain, Ignoring the Cause

When I was being rushed to the emergency room, the pain in my head was so unbearable that all I wanted was for it to go away. This pain, though, was my body's warning system that something was terribly wrong. Without it, I would have continued going about my life oblivious to my illness, until its effects caused permanent damage or even death. This God-given warning system told the doctors where to start examining me and what tests to run in order to determine what was causing my pain.

Because it took a while for the doctors to agree on my diagnosis, they gave me various medications before they found the right combination of drugs to address my illness. Yet once the diagnosis of spinal meningitis was confirmed, I received medication that targeted the direct source of the problem. I also received very powerful painkillers that eased my severe headache, which I discovered is one of the key symptoms of the disease. This respite from pain helped me to rest comfortably while my body was healing. It also enabled me to think more clearly and to pray during my recovery.

LIMITATIONS OF PAINKILLERS

Painkillers are wonderful inventions of the medical field. They take away feelings of discomfort, relieve suffering from accidents and illnesses, allow surgery to be performed, and sometimes even keep patients alive by easing excruciating

93

pain. They also enable people to function in life when they would otherwise be crippled by debilitating illnesses.

But painkillers do have limitations. They are designed to address only the symptoms—not the cause—of the pain. My father received hospice care in my home for a few months before he went home to be with the Lord. He suffered from bone cancer. This disease is agonizingly painful and paralyzes the body. My father sometimes had to take twenty to thirty pills a day and, during the time of his greatest pain, liquid morphine. These painkillers immediately eased his agony, so that, even though he had a devastating, body-destroying disease, he was able to be lucid and have important conversations with his family. He also retained his wonderful sense of humor. Because of the painkillers, my father was made comfortable during the last days of his life.

PAINKILLERS ADDRESS ONLY THE SYMPTOMS, NOT THE CAUSE.

However, even though I was grateful that the medicine was easing his pain, I knew that it could not heal the cancer consuming his body. It could not address the root cause of his pain. Through my father's illness, I saw firsthand both the benefits and limitations of painkillers. Numbing the pain with powerful medicines helps us to cope with physical distress, but these medicines do not *cure* our diseases. They only help us to continue to function as they relieve our symptoms.

WET RAGS AND COPPER PENNIES

As a young girl, I was blessed to have my great-grandmother in my life until I was about fifteen. She was an extraordinarily wise woman who lived to the ripe old age of ninety-nine. "Aunt Sue"—as she was known throughout the family—had hundreds of medicines to "cure whatever ails you." Most of what she knew about "doctoring," as she called it, she learned growing up in the tobacco and cotton fields of North Carolina. Many of her remedies came from things she found around the house or in her backyard garden. Whenever someone in the family became ill, she would go to her garden and come back with a variety of vegetables and herbs. Then she would crush, stir, fix, and mix various ingredients together and come up with some extraordinary concoctions—some of which seemed to work as well as any modern-day medicine. These concoctions were the culmination of many years of folk wisdom and tradition.

I remember that whenever my brothers and sisters and I had childhood fevers, she would not reach for aspirin or any other modern medicine to numb our pain. Instead, Aunt Sue would wet a rag with cold water, place it on our foreheads, and tell us to lie down for thirty minutes and think good thoughts. Then she would tell us to put a copper penny in our shoe and keep it there for an entire day, and the pain of the fever would go away.

I'm not sure if my great-grandmother's medicine really worked or if it only *seemed* to work because she said it would. Sometimes the fever would subside, but it would eventually return, resulting in even more pain, especially if it was caused by a serious condition that needed professional medical intervention.

NUMBING THE FEELING

Just as the more serious illnesses of my brothers and sisters and I needed the attention of a medical doctor, we all have problems in our lives that require serious spiritual attention. Many of these problems are the result of deep emotional wounds that caused us to make poor decisions and act in ways that are self-destructive. Sometimes we are not even aware of the existence of these emotional wounds. We are only aware of the pain they cause. Yet the pain is a warning sign; it is a surface symptom of something that is wrong deep within us.

PAIN IS A WARNING SIGN.

Instead of accepting the more difficult challenge of addressing the root causes of our pain, we concoct ways to merely alleviate our discomfort. We try a variety of things to relieve the pain caused by childhood traumas or events that bring us stress in our daily lives. These "concoctions" are like my great-grandmother's "wet rag and copper penny" because they are well-intended attempts at a cure. They are designed to take away feelings of emotional discomfort and relieve suffering. They help us to function on a daily basis—at least temporarily—by easing excruciating emotional pain that would otherwise cripple us. However, they do not address the deeper root causes of our pain. They only numb our painful feelings.

Pain hurts, but we need to remember that it serves as a wake-up call for us. It is an indicator that something within us is either wrong or not functioning properly. In the same way that a blinding headache signals the presence of a potentially life-threatening disease such as meningitis, emotional pain can be an indication of the presence of serious emotional distress. Later in this chapter, we will discuss some of the concoctions, or self-prescribed "painkillers," we rely on to numb the pain that accompanies serious issues in our lives—issues we find too difficult and stressful to confront.

EMOTIONAL SCARS

I have discovered that many people who seem to be moving through life without a care in the world are suffering from more hurts than most of their friends, associates, and even family members realize. I know that these people are hurting because of the poor choices and repeated destructive behavior patterns in their lives.

Often, the smiles on our faces are covering a flood of tears in our hearts. The pain within us has a variety of causes:

➢ We were given a raw deal at work.
➢ We were belittled by a stranger, relative, or friend.
➢ Our character has been maligned.
➢ We were betrayed by a trusted friend.
➢ We were abused.
➢ We have experienced the devastation of a broken relationship.
➢ We have deep emotional scars stemming from childhood.

Unfortunately, the last cause of pain listed is the one that can produce the most damage. This is because we are often unaware that the trauma exists or that our present thoughts and behaviors are being affected and shaped by events far in the past. These painful experiences from the past are like irritating echoes that keep repeating throughout our lives.

"HEART BURN"

Before we learn to deal with the root causes of our pain, we try to deal with our hurt in one of two ways:

➢ Internalize
➢ Retaliate

Internalized hurt is like "heart burn" that touches us in the deepest places of our souls. We store our internalized hurt feelings in a reserve of unresolved anger. Then these suppressed feelings come out in the form of bitterness, resentment, and hostility toward other people. Those who are always angry—seemingly without provocation—are really revealing their hurting hearts.

Sometimes, people spend their lives trying to retaliate or get even with people who have offended or hurt them. Often the original offender is no longer present, such as a father who abandoned his family or a mother who was emotionally unavailable to her children. At times, people try to deal with this kind of heart burn by erecting an imaginary wall against further wounds. This type of emotional withdrawal is a defense mechanism. It is a "painkiller" people use to protect their fragile hearts at all costs. That is why some people change relationships like a dancer changes partners on a dance floor. Their emotional withdrawal is an attempt to numb themselves against the fear and pain that a broken relationship might bring. It is easier for them to change spouses than to submit to potentially painful but long-lasting spiritual medicine for their hurts, such as prayer, pastoral counseling, and other professional help.

PREEXISTING CONDITIONS

Painful events of the past are like preexisting health conditions that have a profound effect on a person's present circumstances. A patient may go to the doctor's office with a relatively minor medical problem, but the manner in which the doctor addresses the problem will be influenced by other conditions that the patient has. For example, a simple sore on the foot can be life-threatening to a person who is a diabetic. A dab of antiseptic and a bandage is not sufficient to address that patient's problem. This principle is applicable to our spiritual lives and our relationships with others. For instance, when a problem erupts in a marriage in which the husband and wife have preexisting conflicts and unresolved issues, it can cause a major setback in their relationship.

Every other week, I see couples in my office like George and Sheila. When they came to me for counseling, they told me that their marriage had been going great for five years—until Sheila found a photo in her husband's wallet of a woman whom she did not recognize. When she questioned him about it, he became extremely agitated and acted in a suspicious manner. After further counseling, I learned that Sheila had noticed other signs of infidelity in her husband's behavior over the years. After three sessions, George refused to continue the counseling. He concluded that the marital problems he and his wife were experiencing were the result of her prying, inquisitive behavior. He felt that he was somehow entitled to his infidelity, stating, "All men play around," because, while he was growing up, he had observed his father's unfaithfulness to his mother. He was using sexual promiscuity as a painkiller for his unsettling childhood.

UNRESOLVED ISSUES CAN CAUSE A MAJOR SETBACK.

A year later, George and Sheila were filing for divorce. Sheila had discovered that her husband had fathered a child by a woman with whom he had been having a relationship for two years—the same woman whose photo she had found in her husband's wallet. George's way of addressing their marital problems was merely to tell his wife, "Mind your own business."

Infidelity was not the *cause* of the breakdown of their relationship; rather, it was a symptom of a more deeply rooted, preexisting problem from George's childhood and unresolved issues in their marriage. George never dealt with the root cause of his pain, and so he simply moved on to another woman *and* another church. His "solution" was like putting a bandage over a gaping wound and expecting the wound to heal on its own. Unfortunately, some of us deal with trauma in our lives in much the same way. We look for quick fixes and simple answers to anesthetize pain that is very deeply rooted within us.

QUICK FIX

Television commercials and direct mail advertising will tell you there is a pill, a salve, a liquid, a balm, or an injection for everything that ails you. Pharmacies and grocery store aisles are filled with remedies for sleeplessness, weight gain, and smoking. While not all of such medications and health aids are bad, it is much easier for us to pop a pill than to address our negative feelings.

WE WANT A MAGICAL TOUCH FROM GOD.

When we turn to man-made painkillers, we are seeking a quick fix for our adversities. We often feel that we should be healed of a difficulty or crisis in our lives by a magical touch from God. But quick fixes are temporary anesthetics. They remove the pain of our immediate symptoms, but they do not address the cause or issue of the pain itself.

None of us likes physical pain, and we will do almost anything to alleviate the slightest discomfort. Emotional pain is just as disturbing to us as physical pain, although it affects us in a different way. Often it has an even greater overall impact on our lives. Physical pain is readily noticeable, and it causes us to seek immediate relief. However, we can suppress emotional pain for long periods of time and bury it within us so that we are unaware of its existence. Then it becomes difficult for us to acknowledge or address it. Yet the subconscious mind and body can still feel its effects, and its presence in our lives can be devastating. In such cases, we are in danger of serious side effects as the pain ferments within us.

A PILL FOR EVERYTHING

I was watching the local news broadcast one evening when an interesting story caught my attention. The words "medical breakthrough" flashed across the television screen. I listened in amazement as the broadcaster talked about a pill, which is currently available, that can supposedly cure a person struggling with a gambling addiction. "One pill at breakfast with a glass of water is all you need," the reporter said, "to take away the urge to gamble for a full twenty-four hours."

I thought, "How extraordinary and how sad it is to think that the public is being led to believe that a pill can effectively address a problem that obviously has deep emotional roots." Then I thought about how we live in a day and time when we have a pill for just about everything. A pill a day might relieve the urge or the discomfort of a gambling addiction, but no pill or chemical alone can adequately address emotional pain that has been suppressed for long periods of time.

EMOTIONAL TRANQUILIZERS

Medications that cause drowsiness and induce sleep in anxious patients are some of the greatest inventions of modern medicine. They have a soothing, calming, tranquilizing effect. However, used improperly and over an extended period of time, they can damage a person's health. Tranquilizers and sedatives are not meant to alleviate pain. Instead, they are strong chemicals that work in certain areas of the brain to dull the senses so that an individual feels drowsy and calm. When a person is drowsy, he or she is less sensitive to feelings of pain.

Sexual promiscuity, alcohol, illegal drugs, overeating, excessive spending, gambling, and so on, can be used as *emotional* tranquilizers. When we engage in these activities, we are attempting to decrease our ability to "feel" our emotional pain. However, just as all sedatives eventually wear

100

off, when we stop engaging in these destructive behaviors, our emotional pains and stresses return.

Over time, a patient can develop immunities to sedatives and tranquilizers and have to take increased dosages of them to achieve the same effect. In a similar way, after a while, people have to drink more alcohol, use more drugs, and engage in more illicit sexual activity in order to successfully anesthetize themselves against emotional pain.

SYMPTOM RELIEF

George, whom I mentioned earlier, continually buried his emotional pain; he substituted increasingly deeper involvement with another woman for dealing with his problems. I must give George some credit in that he did at first agree to go into counseling with his wife, which is a major step for most men. But when the conversation during the counseling turned to matters he found difficult to discuss, he decided to discontinue the sessions. Many times, individuals will seek help for their emotional pain from Christian counselors; professional agencies; or spiritually mature, trusted friends. After a short period of time, they may feel less stressed and anxious about their situations because of the help they are receiving. Once the pain starts to subside and the symptoms begin to be relieved, the tendency is to discontinue seeking help. However, refusing additional help can be hazardous in the long run.

Doctors continually warn their patients against the tendency to discontinue treatment. Certain infections respond immediately to medications such as penicillin. When patients notice that their symptoms are being relieved, they are tempted to stop taking their medication. Because of this, all prescription medications come with a warning label that says something like, "Continue to take all of this medication, even after symptoms begin to disappear." Doctors know that if patients do not complete their treatments,

WE OFTEN DISCONTINUE SEEKING HELP WHEN THE PAIN BEGINS TO SUBSIDE.

their sicknesses can lie dormant within them and flare up at a later time, causing even greater harm. In other words, the sickness does not go away. The disease-causing organism is merely latent, and the disease is only in remission.

INCOMPLETE TREATMENTS

Sometimes, in our attempts to relieve our symptoms, we apply incomplete treatments that never fully address the root cause of our problems. Emily, the wife of a prominent pastor of a very large church, had been in a state of psychological numbness for over twenty years. She shared with me how she had suffered in silence all those years, enduring physical abuse from her husband. She also revealed that there was a history of physical abuse in her own family of origin.

Emily had been saved as a child and had been active in the church all her life. She told me that she had done all the "right things" to address the trauma of abuse. She had studied the Word of God. She had prayed. She had even gone for spiritual counsel several times—but whenever her husband found out about it, he prevented her from continuing.

Her situation seemed to improve for a time, and she thought everything was fine until she suffered a horrible beating from her husband, which landed her in the hospital with a broken arm. Since that time, she had been experiencing panic attacks as well as other symptoms, such as dizziness, headaches, gastrointestinal problems, and insomnia. Emily could not understand why she was still experiencing such devastating physical abuse and its resulting problems. She was a Christian woman who had been praying and fasting. After all she had done, how could God allow her to be a battered wife?

I told Emily that God takes no glory out of our being brutalized. In 1 Corinthians 7:15, Paul gave us a principle for abuse situations such as Emily's. He said, *"God has called us to peace."* Since her husband refused to stop abusing her, I counseled her to decide on a specific plan for her life and to leave. That was surely a "bitter pill" for her to swallow—but she would have to swallow it in order to save her life. Some Christians may not agree with the counsel I gave her, but I believed that in Emily's case it was a life-preserving measure and that God would not judge a woman for leaving her husband when she was being brutally abused. She had already been so badly beaten that she had needed to go to the hospital. I could not simply give her a list of Bible verses and tell her that if she would go home and repeat them three times a day, her problems would all go away. The *strong medicine* she needed may seem harsh, but it was necessary to preserve her life.

I explained to Emily that she—and her husband—needed to examine the root causes of his violence, and that her tolerance of such behavior needed to be examined, as well. She had received faulty teaching about what the Bible intends by the concept of submission, and she had resigned herself to her way of life. Therefore, she had always suffered her abuse in silence and had buried her pain. Whenever she had sustained bruises or other injuries from being beaten, she had always covered them with her clothing or made up a story to explain them away. Although she was a victim, she was also an enabler of her husband's problem because she never tried to put a stop to his abuse.

In answer to Emily's question about why she was still experiencing difficulties after reading the Bible, praying and fasting, and going for counseling, I explained that the Word of God is not meant to be used like a narcotic, which lulls a person to sleep and is used by some for the purpose of avoiding the harsh realities of life. Neither is it a "magic pill" that makes our problems disappear. Instead of using the Word as a magic potion, Emily needed to apply the Word to her life so that it could strengthen her and give her the courage to protect herself and endure what people might think or say if she left her abusive situation. In addition, prayer is not to be used like a ritual, as if merely saying the right words will bring the desired results. God's answer to our prayers and seeking His guidance may be that we have to do something active to address our circumstances. Emily's prayers needed to focus on the very real need to preserve her life and the lives of her children and on looking into the root causes of her problems.

Moreover, counseling is necessary, good, and beneficial, but it is not a complete treatment in itself. All human problems have spiritual roots. Counseling generally addresses our symptoms, but the Word of God addresses the *spirit* behind the root causes of our symptoms. We must discover and address these spiritual roots if the progress of spiritual disease is to be reversed and eradicated and if the "patient" is to be fully delivered. Six months of counseling might help to relieve our symptoms, but our difficulties will not be solved if we do not address these underlying causes. An integration of both counseling *and* guidance from the *strong medicine* of the Word of God is essential.

We need to recognize that it takes time to truly examine core issues in our lives. Sometimes it takes six weeks for certain medications to begin to work, and even after they start to show results, they need to be maintained on a long-term basis. Similarly, turning your life over to God is just the beginning of your growth in Christ. Your salvation is sealed and secure, but the process of your spiritual growth must be initiated, carried out, and maintained over a lifetime.

In Emily's case, the wise thing was for her to remove herself from the abusive situation. There would be a greater opportunity for her husband to recognize his error and receive help by her leaving than by her staying and continuing to enable his problem—with the possibility of being permanently injured or killed in the process. Perhaps what was most painful for Emily is that she saw the spirit of violence developing in her children as they modeled their father's behavior. Yet in order for her to swallow the bitter pill of leaving, she had to face her worst fear: being the single mother of a broken family. Emily's strong medicine was difficult to take, but taking it was the right and responsible thing for herself, her children—and her husband.

Many times we also try applying incomplete treatments to our adversities by doing good things, such as praying and reading the Bible, but failing to apply the full treatment: a combination of studying the Word of God, prayer, solid counsel, and taking action as God directs us and as is wise and expedient for the situation.

DESPERATE MEASURES

A surface cut, left untreated, will probably heal on its own, and the evidence of such a minor abrasion will fade

over a period of time. However, a deep wound requires serious, extensive medical attention. The physical pain that a
surface cut causes is barely noticeable, but a serious wound
can cause such unbearable pain that a person will resort to
unthinkable measures in order to alleviate it.

This truth reminds me of a man I read about who was
trapped in an overturned car after a horrible automobile accident. The man lay in the twisted wreckage undiscovered for
two days before he was rescued. His body had been con-
torted in the accident, and he was in excruciating pain. One
of his hands became numb, and in a desperate attempt to
lessen the pain and save his own life, he used a pocket knife
to sever his left hand.

Likewise, we resort to desperate measures when we use
painkillers to lessen the overwhelming pain of our emotional
wounds. These are futile attempts at ensuring our own emotional survival. Sometimes, our internal pain can be so intense that we become numb to our own feelings. But its
presence is evident by the negative behavior and poor
choices we make, which can have devastating consequences
for our relationships and the entire course of our lives.

These painkillers cause tremendous problems in our
spiritual lives. Whenever we see a person in the body of
Christ falling into various temptations, secretly engaging in
ungodly activities, or repeating patterns of self-destructive
behavior, we automatically label them as "backsliders" and
categorize their actions as "fallen," "ungodly," or "sinful" behavior. Almost without exception, these are people who have
given their lives to Christ but have not surrendered to the
full treatment of God's prescription for a blessed and successful life.

TEMPORARY AIDS TO HEALING

Certain drugs, such as codeine, are potentially addictive,
and physicians prescribe them usually on a short-term basis
only. Many people have become addicted to prescription
drugs after using them to alleviate physical pain, because
they have come to depend on their sedative effect.

Some painkillers can become ineffective over time because the patient's body develops a tolerance to them. If the

drug is the only medicine or the best medicine available for a specific problem, and the illness causing the pain becomes worse, then more and more of the medication is needed to bring relief. However, large dosages of pain medication can cause additional damage or even death in a patient.

Pain medications, then, keep us anesthetized from pain for only short periods of time. They do not cure physical problems, but are only a temporary aid to healing. Moreover, their side effects can be inconvenient, damaging, and in some cases, deadly. *Painkillers are not a long-term solution to illness.*

In the same way, negative patterns and destructive behavior can become addictive over time, because a hurting person comes to depend upon their sedative effect while becoming increasingly tolerant of using them to alleviate emotional pain. If the original problem causing the pain becomes worse, thereby increasing the level of distress, then the person engages in more and more destructive behavior. Yet ungodly behavior can keep a person anesthetized from deep emotional pain for only short periods of time. It is only a temporary aid to emotional healing, and its side effects can be life-damaging.

SELF-MEDICATION

When a person tries to address physical symptoms without the advice of a medical expert, he or she is attempting *self-medication.* We do the same thing when we ignore the wisdom and strength we could receive through prayer and God's Word, and turn to weak substitutes instead. There are a variety of self-medications that we as human beings draw from to try to ease painful problems in our lives. We may try to assuage our pain by comforting ourselves with sensual pleasures. Blaming others for our problems is another strategy we use to anesthetize ourselves. Or we may try to repress our pain by refusing to acknowledge it and pushing it far down inside ourselves or by plunging into hard work in order to drive it from our minds.

GOD OFFERS US COMFORT, STRENGTH, HOPE, AND FAITH.

SENSUAL PLEASURES

Overeating, alcoholism, television addiction, obsession with sports, pornography, and substance abuse all can be symptoms of attempts at self-medication. People turn to food, drink, sex, and other "painkillers" because they think these things will soothe their inner distresses.

For example, as in George's case, if a person is having marital problems, he or she may try to self-medicate by changing spouses or sinking into a diversion, such as alcohol, drug addiction, or infidelity, instead of getting to the root cause of the issues of difficulties in relationships.

Self-medication might seem to work for a while, but it soon becomes evident to those who attempt it that the help is only temporary and the side effects can be damaging. Before long, people also start building immunities to these false supports, so that they need more and more quantities of them to ease the pain that rises from their hearts. This "overmedication" can cause serious problems.

Sometimes, people may try to fix the secondary problems and negative side effects they have created for themselves in their attempts to self-medicate. However, instead of finally addressing their real issues, they will often force themselves to change through diets, abstinence, or other forms of self-discipline. Restraint and self-discipline can bring some good results; however, if the original problem that drove them to self-medicate is never addressed, the pain will resurface in some form or other, sooner or later.

For instance, if a person has used food as a painkiller and is now struggling with a weight problem, he or she might cut out sweets or go on a fad diet and lose thirty pounds. However, if the feelings of pain, fear, or loneliness that prompted the use of food as an anesthetic in the first place are never addressed, he or she may go in the opposite direction and end up with a serious health problem like anorexia in an attempt to cope with the pain while avoiding weight gain.

BLAMING OTHERS

Anger and resentment can be types of painkillers because they are attempts to release pain by transferring it to someone else. When we lash out at others in anger, or allow anger to smolder inside us, we may be revealing our inner self-hatred, guilt, sadness, or doubt. We unconsciously think that if someone else can be blamed for the bad feelings we are experiencing, we will not have to go through the painful process of confronting our own hurts and disappointments. Many people who display anger toward others in situations are really covering up deep feelings of fear and anxiety. Fear can cause us to act and react in ways that are inappropriate and irrational. The enemy then builds on our fear to cause us to make unwise choices and foolish decisions.

"Snake Oil" Medicine

It is bad enough when we attempt to self-medicate and end up causing ourselves more harm than good. However, sometimes when we turn to others for "pain medicine" in dealing with difficult life issues—especially those we consider our spiritual leaders—we can receive extremely flawed advice that can have devastating side effects. I am not saying that we should blame our spiritual counselors when things do not seem to work out in our lives. Rather, I am referring to instances where those who are supposed to be our spiritual leaders or mature Christians have a faulty understanding of God's Word or promote false teaching—causing disastrous results in the lives and relationships of those they counsel.

FALSE TEACHING CAN CAUSE DISASTROUS RESULTS.

Years ago, there used to be traveling medicine shows, in which salesmen would tout all-purpose remedies to naive customers. This medicine was usually worthless, yet it was supposed to cure all kinds of ailments. People would trust these salesmen, who sold what came to be known as "snake oil," because they believed the salesmen were knowledgeable; they thought they would obtain the promised cure. Likewise, many people automatically believe everything preachers or teachers tell them and do not take the responsibility of prayerfully searching through the Word of God and studying what they are being taught. They just swallow whatever is fed to them. Not all who preach or teach error do so knowingly or willfully. However, the Bible instructs us to search the Scriptures to test what others teach us. (See Acts 17:11; 1 Thessalonians 5:21.)

TOXIC TEACHING

An example of faulty teaching about adversity that has caused many heartaches is the view that wives must "submit" to their husbands at all costs no matter what their husbands require them to do. This is the advice that distressed wives are sometimes given by pastors and other Christians when they seek help for painful problems in their marriages. The advice they receive ends up being "snake oil" that, when applied to their problems, not only does not heal but also introduces toxic teaching into their lives.

I once counseled a young Christian mother who was having a great deal of difficulty in her marriage with her Christian husband. When I talked with this young mother, she told me that her husband had learned from their former pastor that he was the "boss" of his home and that this was the teaching of the Bible. "What can I do with my husband?" she said. "I can't do anything without his okay. He treats me more like a child than his wife. Is this God's will for my life?"

A large number of misteachings about the relationship between husbands and wives have been taught over the years to the body of Christ. Some of these misteachings have been the result of ignorance. Sadly, others have been promoted for the purpose of strengthening the low opinion many men in the church have had of women or to justify masculine insecurities about women. These insecurities have been built upon the false premise that woman alone and not man was responsible for sin and death entering the world. The absolute authority of men, submissive women, hierarchical headship, and marital subjugation are irrevocable and indisputable Bible doctrines in some denominations. The idea is that Eve disobeyed her husband's authority when she sinned, and therefore women are forced into a permanent secondary role.

These views do not reflect God's original design in the creation of man and woman, which Christ redeemed at the cross:

"Let Us make [humankind] *in Our image, according to Our likeness; let them have dominion over the fish of the sea, over the birds of the air, and over the cattle, over all the earth and over every creeping thing that creeps on the earth." So God created* [humankind] *in His own image; in the image of God He created him; male and female He created them.*
(Genesis 1:26–27)

Quite frankly, a Christian husband with a healthy sense of who he is in God has no desire to have his wife "submit" to him without fully submitting to her as well. The Christian pattern is one of mutual submission and love. (See Ephesians 5:21–28.) In a healthy, Christ-centered, Word-centered marriage, husband and wife are best friends, and friendship and personal growth cannot exist where one feels entitled to exercise control over the other. A strong Christian marriage is a partnership. More than that, it is a "trinity," where Jesus Christ is the third person and is absolute Lord.

"QUACKS"

When the western United States was still being settled, there were people who roamed the countryside claiming to be doctors. They carried with them bottled mixtures of potions and powders that they touted as medicines and cure-alls. These so-called doctors were frauds because they had neither the knowledge nor the expertise to practice medicine. They were also deceptive because, although they didn't really intend to harm anyone, they *knew* they had no real medical knowledge. As a result, their advice was often deadly. These people became known as "quacks," a term taken from the archaic word *quacksalver*, which means "one who pretends to have medical knowledge." They were even worse than the snake oil salesmen because they didn't just sell questionable medicines but also boasted of having medical expertise and engaged in activities that were potentially life-threatening to

110

people. Claiming to be competent, quacks did much more harm than good in their efforts to help.

In a similar way, sometimes the advice we receive from "counselors" as godly teaching is really a mixture of fact and fiction combined with the individuals' personal hang-ups and ego problems. Misguided counsel and fraudulent advice is so damaging because the "religious quacks" who dispense it usually *know* they are giving out false teaching. They know they are using the Word of God merely to further their own ideas and prejudices.

A woman who was concerned over her husband's infidelity was told by a "Christian" marriage counselor that if she would submit to her husband and do whatever he wanted her to do, God would be pleased and everything would work out wonderfully. This woman ended up contracting the AIDS virus from her husband and dying. I use this illustration because it is a reality and clearly demonstrates that we have to be careful about the advice we accept from others. The Word of God should not be used like snake oil, casually applied to people's real-life situations. Moreover, what may be appropriate in one person's situation may not be appropriate for another person when all factors are taken into consideration.

WE MUST BE CAREFUL ABOUT THE ADVICE WE RECEIVE.

Another example of false teaching about our adversities is the idea that our problems do not really exist—that if we do not "confess" them, they will have no effect on us. While it is true that there is great power in the thoughts we think, and that we are to apply strong faith to all situations, the Bible never tells us to ignore our problems or deny that they exist. In 2 Corinthians 4:8–9, Paul declared, *"We are hard pressed on every side, yet not crushed; we are perplexed, but not in despair; persecuted, but not forsaken; struck down, but not destroyed."* In this passage, he admitted his struggles, but he also acknowledged his faith and hope that God would give him victory.

If we are taught to ignore the existence of our problems, we will be less likely to actively commit them to God and see how He causes all things to work together for our good. We may miss a great opportunity to witness God at work in the midst of our trials. We may also be in danger of turning to false painkillers as we try to cope with the reality of our pain without directly addressing or acknowledging it.

The tragic outcome of such teaching is illustrated by the thinking of Mary Baker Eddy, founder of Christian Science. Christian Science teaches that sin, sickness, and death are created by our minds. Mrs. Eddy, who died in 1910, arranged to have a telephone installed in her coffin so that when her mind overcame the delusion of death, she could call her associates and be retrieved from her grave. The call has not yet been made, and never will. Sin, sickness, and death are realities in human experience. Yet Christ has gained the victory over them. Peter said,

> *Blessed be the God and Father of our Lord Jesus Christ, who according to His abundant mercy has begotten us again to a living hope through the resurrection of Jesus Christ from the dead, to an inheritance incorruptible and undefiled and that does not fade away.* (1 Peter 1:3–4)

WE ARE ACCOUNTABLE

These examples of misteaching caution us that it is ultimately our responsibility to guard against faulty painkillers that others try to administer to us. We must take control over our own care by searching the Word of God for ourselves as we work through various issues. The people who purchased snake oil years ago trusted in the salesman's supposed knowledge. Yet it is our responsibility to test what people are saying and not just swallow anything that is handed to us. It is very important that we make ourselves accountable to learn the Word of God and apply it to our lives instead of just having the preacher or teacher spoon-feed it to us. We shouldn't swallow anything without carefully examining it.

When you go to another Christian for advice, remember to be sure that the person is someone you can trust to give you advice based on the Word of God. We have to make sure that we are being fed the pure, unadulterated Word that provides true healing. God's Word brings inspiration from God to our lives—not division and destruction. Make sure you are not being fed opinion, prejudice, or tradition. If you are a "baby" Christian who has just recently committed your life to the Lord, you may need assistance in feeding on the Word, but the food you are eating still needs to be healthy. Moreover, it is never too early to read and study the Bible yourself in order to fill your heart and mind with God's Word. If fact, it is essential to your spiritual growth. This does not mean that you do not need to receive solid Bible teaching from qualified teachers and preachers who teach the undiluted Word of God. It just means that you also need to be knowledgeable about God's Word so that you are able to test what you hear about God from others.

AVOID FAULTY OPINIONS AND EMPTY TRADITION.

In contrast to a generation ago, there are people in the pew who study as much as some people in the pulpit. This is a good thing because we are becoming more Word-centered as opposed to merely passing down what traditionalism says is true. We must regard assumptions, long-standing traditions, and private interpretations with caution and compare them with what we read in Scripture.

Another good practice in avoiding faulty teaching is to attend a Bible study. Some of us live on just what we hear during Sunday morning worship. But absorbing whatever is given to us can be a dangerous practice. There is a difference between hearing and really *listening to* and *examining* the Word. Midweek Bible study is the time when we can ask questions, zero in on problem areas, and get into discussions where we work through issues.

It is clear, then, that we need to stop anesthetizing ourselves with man-made painkillers and relying on "snake oil" advice. When we use false painkillers, we reveal our bewilderment and desperation to find lasting relief from our suffering. Our desire to be free from pain is natural. Yet God wants to provide us with His healing balm for our pain as He brings us through our adversities.

PAIN IS A BUILT-IN INDICATOR

In the natural realm, pain actually does us much good. First, it is a red flag. It is a built-in indicator that there is a problem to be addressed. Pain aids us in our diagnosis of illness or injury by helping us locate the source of the problem.

Second, pain warns us against going beyond a certain threshold. For example, if you were to stick a pin in your finger, the pain would let you know when to stop before causing injury. It is when we ignore the warning signs and push ourselves beyond pain's threshold that we can get into trouble.

Third, pain is a protective mechanism. There are sensory nerves on the surface of the skin that protect the body. If you were to accidentally touch a hot stove, you would experience the involuntary reaction of drawing your hand back. If you did not have pain's built-in protection, you might leave your hand on the stove and suffer a third-degree burn. If you never felt the pain of the burn and didn't care for it, the burn might even become infected and lead to additional complications.

Another way pain protects is by keeping us from continuing an activity that could be detrimental or injurious to us. If you sprain your ankle, the pain you experience tells you that you should allow your ankle to heal and not continue walking on it.

Similar principles of pain apply to your spiritual life. Mental, emotional, and spiritual pain tell you when there is a problem or issue to be addressed. They warn you that certain activities and actions are harmful to you, and they protect you from hurting yourself further by letting you know you should stop participating in harmful activities. When you use man-made painkillers to mask your pain, you are blocking this natural mechanism that God has built into you to protect and warn you. Pain of any form is never pleasant, but it can be very beneficial.

Keep in mind that God usually puts a limit on our pain and times of trial. Yet for the time that God allows adversity in your life, it is very important that you learn the lessons and gain the knowledge that He wants you to receive.

Another point to consider is that there is always some pain before the birth of a child. The pain you are experiencing may be "labor pains" of something very worthwhile that will be "birthed" into your life, which will ultimately bring you joy. Ask God to use your pain to birth something good in your life, and see what God brings forth. Jesus said,

> *A woman, when she is in labor, has sorrow because her hour has come; but as soon as she has given birth to the child, she no longer remembers the anguish, for joy that a human being has been born into the world. Therefore you now have sorrow; but I will see you again and your heart will rejoice, and your joy no one will take from you.* (John 16:21–22)

FINDING THE REAL CURE

To find the real cure for our difficulties, we cannot just numb the pain and ignore its cause. We must address both the pain and its source if we are to apply God's *strong medicine* and receive His healing. The chapters that follow will examine our spiritual prognosis and provide *prescriptions for successful living.*

The Bible mentions a man named Jabez, the head of a family in Judah, and a descendent of King David. Jabez' name meant "sorrow," but he looked to God to help him move beyond his sorrow and into blessing. His life is an illustration to us that pain is not an end in itself, but that God wants to use its presence in our lives to bless us.

> *And Jabez was more honourable than his brethren: and his mother called his name Jabez, saying, Because I bare him with sorrow ["pain," NKJV]. And Jabez called on the God of Israel, saying, Oh that thou wouldest bless me indeed, and enlarge my coast, and that thine hand might be with me, and that thou wouldest keep me from evil, **that it may not grieve me**! And God granted him that which he requested.* (1 Chronicles 4:9–10 KJV, emphasis added)

The New King James Version translates verse ten as, *"That I may not **cause** pain!"* (emphasis added).

115

The presence of pain in our lives is not to grieve us, but to bring us to God so that we may receive His comfort, help, strength, and purposes. In our difficulties, we do not need to bear our pain alone or cause pain in others by lashing out at them in anger over our circumstances. We can cry out to God, and He will answer and use even our pain to bring about great good in our lives and the lives of others.

Let us always keep in mind that pain is the result of the fact that we live in a fallen world. But God has the last word on pain, and in it He gives us this promise:

> *And God will wipe away every tear from their eyes; there shall be no more death, nor sorrow, nor crying. There shall be no more pain, for the former things have passed away.* (Revelation 21:4)

I invite you to pray this prayer as you acknowledge your pain and offer it to God to use for His purposes:

> *Lord, I no longer desire to anesthetize my pain, because it keeps me from acknowledging the real issues in my life. You know the pain that I am experiencing, and You know how much it hurts. Help me to have the courage to face both my pain and my difficult circumstance so that I may address the true source of the problem and enter into Your healing. Amen.*

 ## SPIRITUAL VITAMINS

❑ Set aside some time this week to write down your feelings about the difficulty you are experiencing and the pain that it has brought you. Then offer your life and your difficulty to God, acknowledging that He will use even this situation for your good and His glory.

❑ For the next week, pray the prayer at the end of chapter four so that you can acknowledge your pain to God and begin the process of receiving the grace and blessing He wants to give you through your circumstance.

❑ Read and memorize these verses, so that you will have God's perspective on your pain and suffering:

Now no chastening seems to be joyful for the present, but painful; nevertheless, afterward it yields the peaceable fruit of righteousness to those who have been trained by it. Therefore strengthen the hands which hang down, and the feeble knees, and make straight paths for your feet, so that what is lame may not be dislocated, but rather be healed.
(Hebrews 12:11–13)

And God will wipe away every tear from their eyes; there shall be no more death, nor sorrow, nor crying. There shall be no more pain, for the former things have passed away. (Revelation 21:4)

5

PROGNOSIS

Predicting the Outcome

It is amazing how much our lives can change in just a short period of time. When I was recovering in the hospital, I thought about how, just days earlier, I had been busy taking care of my children, pastoring my church, and planning a variety of new endeavors—while all the time my body was being attacked by a serious disease. I had not exhibited all of the symptoms of spinal meningitis, and therefore I had not known I should seek treatment. By the time I got to the hospital, the disease was in an advanced stage. My body had been trying to fight the meningitis all the time the disease was progressing, but I was not aware of it.

As I lay in my hospital bed, I pondered the events of the previous week, starting with my frantic ride to the hospital for medical help. I thought about how I might have lost my life that day in the emergency room. I thanked God from my heart for enabling me to get to the hospital on time so that my illness could be treated and brought under control. I told Him how much I appreciated the strength He had given me to determine to live and fulfill the purposes He had for my life.

MY PHYSICAL PROGNOSIS

My thoughts then turned to my recovery. Doctors refer to a patient's prospect of recovery as a *prognosis.* It is a prediction of a patient's ability to recover based on the doctors' medical knowledge and past experience with similar cases. As a result of God's healing strength, the doctors' accurate diagnosis of my condition, and the administration of the appropriate medication, I was now out of danger, and the prospect of my physical recovery was very good. I still had a long way to go before I would fully recover. Weeks of rest and recuperation lay ahead of me. However, I felt I was making real progress when certain medical treatments were suspended because the disease had been brought under control.

After a few days in the intensive care unit, I was noticeably stronger, and about the fifth day, I was moved to separate division of intensive care. I was not taken to a general ward where there would be a large number of patients to be cared for, but was kept in a step-down unit because the doctors wanted to make sure that my condition was stable. My good prognosis was dependent upon not only the initial critical care I received but also on my follow-up treatment.

For the first few days I had been at the highest level of care the hospital provided, but now I could receive a secondary level of care because my condition was no longer life-threatening and my healing was progressing. Based on their knowledge of the usual course of spinal meningitis and the way my body was responding to the medicine, the doctors were satisfied that my progress was good, and they knew what treatments to give me as I was recovering.

The care I received was still very focused and specific. I continued to receive medications that directly targeted my illness, but the doctors did not see me as regularly as they had at first. The nurses continued to monitor my progress, but they did not check on me every half hour as they had previously. I still had medications administered intravenously and certain machines monitoring my progress, but other machines—such as the heart monitor and nasal cannula that delivers oxygen—were no longer needed. I was on my way to a full recovery.

MY SPIRITUAL PROGNOSIS

However, as I was recuperating in the hospital, God was speaking to my spirit, and I knew that I actually had two prognoses to consider: a physical one and a spiritual one. My physical prognosis would continue to be extremely good if I followed the attending physician's orders and kept taking the prescribed medicine. Yet what about the spiritual truths that God had been showing me and the greater intimacy with Him that I had experienced? What were the chances for their continued progress in my life after I returned to my busy schedule? How could I continue to learn more about God and go to the next level of spiritual maturity so that my spiritual prognosis would also remain excellent?

Before I found myself in the emergency room with a serious illness, I could not have predicted my ordeal or what God would teach me through it. I did not know He would use a physical ailment to move me to a greater level of intimacy

WHAT WERE MY CHANCES FOR A GOOD SPIRITUAL PROGNOSIS?

with Him and deeper spiritual maturity. But while I could not have predicted my sickness or how God would use it in my life, my knowledge of the Word of God assured me that I could predict my spiritual prognosis. The doctors used their medical knowledge and past experience with similar cases to determine my chances of recovery from spinal meningitis. In a similar way, the principles of the Bible and its record of the experiences of God's people would show me my likelihood of continued spiritual victory.

I knew that God has a plan for my life, as He has for all believers, and that He uses *everything* that happens to me to fulfill His purposes. Therefore, I knew that my spiritual prognosis would remain excellent if I kept the following things in mind and applied them to my specific situation:

Rx God's *promises* to me as His child

Rx God's *perspective* on my adversity

Rx God's *provisions* for my spiritual well-being

Rx God's *plan* for my growth in spiritual maturity

No matter what trial you are facing, an excellent spiritual prognosis is available to you as a child of God. He will use your difficulty to deepen your intimacy with Him and move you to greater levels of faith and spiritual development. In this way, you will be able to love Him more, serve Him more, and become more like Him. Your prognosis will continue to be excellent as you keep the following truths in mind and apply them to your difficulties.

GOD'S PROMISES

It is so important for us to read, learn, memorize, and internalize the promises that God has given us in His Word, because through our application of them we will receive the mind and nature of Christ. This will enable us to live confident, overcoming lives even in the midst of adversity.

> *His divine power has given to us all things that pertain to life and godliness, through the knowledge of Him who called us by glory and virtue, by which have been given to us exceedingly* **great and precious promises, that through these you may be partakers of the divine nature.**
> (2 Peter 1:3–4, emphasis added)

God has given us some particularly *"precious promises"* concerning our trials and tribulations. We can completely depend on His deliverance, His faithfulness, and His guidance.

His Deliverance

Life's problems always seem to go from bad to worse. God is the only One who can reverse this downward spiral. He can take our problems and turn them into glorious victories. Yet there is one necessary requirement: like the psalmist, we must cry out, "Come, Lord, and show me Your mercy."

> *Turn Yourself to me, and have mercy on me, for I am desolate and afflicted. The troubles of my heart have enlarged; bring me out of my distresses!*
> (Psalm 25:16–17)

121

When you are willing to cry out to God, the worst problem can be transformed into something marvelous in Him. He has already made His offer of transformation, but the next step is yours. Invite God into your situation *today.*

Our spiritual prognosis as believers undergoing adversity can be summed up in a Scripture passage that has become priceless to me:

> *The righteous cry out, and the LORD hears, and delivers them out of all their troubles. The LORD is near to those who have a broken heart, and saves such as have a contrite spirit. Many are the afflictions of the righteous, but the LORD delivers him out of them all.*   (Psalm 34:17–19)

God Hears You

"The righteous cry out, and the LORD hears, and delivers them out of all their troubles." God promises to hear the cries of those who call out to Him in the midst of their distress. *"The righteous"* does not refer to those who are "perfect," but to those who belong to God and who seek Him and desire to obey Him.

Your heartfelt cries will not be carried off by the wind. They will not fall on deaf ears. Psalm 116:1–2 says, "I love the LORD, because He has heard My voice and my supplications. Because He has inclined His ear to me, therefore I will call upon Him as long as I live." God not only hears you, He "inclines His ear" to you. When we want to hear something that is being said, we bend our heads in the direction of the speaker so that we will not miss anything. In the same way, God "bends His head in your direction" to hear every word you say.

GOD PROMISES YOU HIS CONSTANT PRESENCE.

God Is Near You

"The LORD is near to those who have a broken heart, and saves such as have a contrite spirit." When adversity is breaking your heart, you can rely on the fact that God is with you and will save you from your troubles as you look to Him for help. God promises you His constant presence—in

the "bad" times as well as in the "good" times. He does not stay at a distance from us. Paul said in Acts 17:27, *"He is not far from each one of us."* In spite of the inevitable struggles and crises that we face, we are not alone. Jesus said, *"These things I have spoken to you, that in Me you may have peace. In the world you will have tribulation; but be of good cheer, I have overcome the world"* (John 16:33).

Remember that one of the names of the Holy Spirit is *Paraclete,* which comes from a Greek word meaning "one called alongside." God comes alongside you as Counselor, Intercessor, and Helper in your time of need. Psalm 145:18–19 says, *"The LORD is near to all who call upon Him, to all who call upon Him in truth. He will fulfill the desire of those who fear Him; He also will hear their cry and save them."*

God Will Deliver You

"Many are the afflictions of the righteous, but the LORD delivers him out of them all." This last verse of the Scripture passage from Psalm 34 gives you two guarantees: (1) You will experience many afflictions; (2) the Lord will deliver you out of them all. It does not tell you that you will avoid experiencing trials or that once you've experienced one trial, you won't ever experience another. However, the tremendous promise to you in this verse is that the Lord *Himself* will deliver you. The prophet Isaiah declared, *"Oh, that You would rend the heavens! That You would come down!"* (Isaiah 64:1). In a sense, that is what God will do for you. In His perfect timing, when He is ready to deliver you, nothing will stand in His way. He will "part the heavens" and come down to rescue you from your troubles.

Not only that, but God will also deliver you from *all* your afflictions as you depend on Him. After Peter declared that satan is a *"roaring lion, seeking whom he may devour"* (1 Peter 5:8), he then said, *"But may the God of all grace, who called us to His eternal glory by Christ Jesus, after you have suffered a while, perfect, establish, strengthen, and settle you"* (v. 10). Peter's prayer for the first-century believers— that God would perfect, establish, strengthen, and settle them—is also God's guarantee to you today. You will come through all your difficulties stronger, wiser, and closer to God.

Remember that God may bring help from unexpected sources, and realize that His deliverance can take a variety of forms. He may take you around your adversity, over your adversity, or right through it. Yet whichever way He delivers you, you can know that He is *"mighty to save"* (Isaiah 63:1).

His Faithfulness

Another precious promise for times of adversity is given by the Lord Jesus: *"I will never leave you nor forsake you"* (Hebrews 13:5). In this declaration, Jesus promises you that
no matter what the conditions,
regardless of the enormity of the problem,
in spite of "impossible" circumstances,
against overwhelming odds,
He will always be with you. *Always.*

God Will Never Leave You

"I will never leave you." God is faithfully working out His purposes in the midst of your adversities, even when you do not recognize that He is there. Sometimes, when God delivers us, it may seem as if He is coming on the scene for the first time, because we do not always *sense* His presence while we are undergoing trials. Yet recall the words of Psalm 34:18, *"The LORD is near to those who have a broken heart, and saves such as have a contrite spirit."* You can know that God is with you even when it seems as if He is absent, because He has *promised* you He will be with you. He will never abandon you.

God Will Never Forsake You

"I will never...forsake you." Jesus will not only stay by your side, but also give you His full attention. He will never become distracted by other people and circumstances. He will never stop helping you, leaving you to figure things out on your own. Jesus will not say to you, "I quit" and walk away. Proverbs 18:24 says, *"There is a friend who sticks closer than a brother."* Jesus is that Friend.

His Guidance

God also gives you the tremendous promise that He will direct your paths—even when your paths are rocky ones.

> Trust in the LORD with all your heart, and lean not on your own understanding; in all your ways acknowledge Him, and He shall direct your paths.
>
> (Proverbs 3:5–6)

God Can Be Trusted

"Trust in the LORD with all your heart." You can trust God completely in the midst of your trials because He is totally dependable. "Who among you fears the LORD? Who obeys the voice of His Servant? Who walks in darkness and has no light? Let him trust in the name of the LORD and rely upon his God" (Isaiah 50:10). We know people are trustworthy when they tell us the truth and when they do what they promise to do. Everything God tells you is true, and what He says He will do, He will perform. "For I am the LORD. I speak, and the word which I speak will come to pass" (Ezekiel 12:25). Jesus assured His disciples—and all of us—that His words are true when He said, "If it were not so, I would have told you" (John 14:2). God will always tell you the truth.

God's Understanding Is Totally Reliable

"Lean not on your own understanding." Your understanding of your adversities is limited to your knowledge, your past experiences, and your present circumstances. You should depend on these resources only to an extent, because you are not to "lean" on them. When you lean on something, you put your entire weight on it. You rely on it to support you. God's understanding is limitless. "As the heavens are higher than the earth, so are My ways higher than your ways, and My thoughts than your thoughts" (Isaiah 55:9). God's knowledge, experience, and power are infinitely greater than yours, and that is why you can rely with complete confidence on His understanding of your circumstances, rather than on your own understanding. You can lean on Him, and He will not let you fall.

LEAN ON GOD.

God Knows Your Ways

"*In all your ways acknowledge Him.*" It is much easier to acknowledge the goodness of the Lord when things are going well. The test of faith is to acknowledge God's goodness during adversity, recognizing that satan, not God, is the source of your pain, and that it is God's strength that will enable you to endure.

Times of adversity are also good opportunities to make certain that you are acknowledging God in all areas of your life. Are you withholding from God any praise that He deserves for blessing and prospering you in your family life, your job, and your talents? Are you relying on your own capabilities rather than on His strength? When you acknowledge God in "*all your ways,*" you can have the assurance that "*the LORD shall preserve your going out and your coming in from this time forth, and even forevermore*" (Psalm 121:8). Because He knows all your ways better than you do, He is the best One to guide you both in times of ease and in times of trouble.

God Will Direct Your Paths

"*He shall direct your paths.*" The end result of trusting in the Lord wholeheartedly, leaning on His understanding, and acknowledging Him in all your ways is that He will "*direct your paths.*" He will guide you and set you in the right direction to fulfill the plan He has for your life and to lead you to His place of deliverance.

It is important to remember that faith comes alive at the point at which we apply Scripture to our lives. Hold fast to all the above promises, and you will build your faith for the spiritual blessings God has for you in the midst of your trials.

GOD'S PERSPECTIVE

God says we can have a positive spiritual prognosis not only by holding fast in faith to His promises but also by viewing our problems from His perspective. One of the best ways to gain God's perspective on your situation is to read the examples of those in the Bible who have undergone trials. Just as doctors look to past medical cases to determine a patient's physical prognosis, the experiences of God's people as they have gone through adversity are like "case studies" that will give you instruction and enlightenment about your own difficulties.

No New Problems

There are really no "new" problems. There are many examples of people in Bible times who struggled with the same things we struggle with: unforgiveness, bitterness, fear, low self-esteem, and broken relationships. Not much has changed over the years. From Adam and Eve to the apostle Peter to us today, humankind has struggled with a variety of spiritual ailments that only God can cure.

The people of the Bible were men and women, young and old, rich and poor, bond and free, king and pauper, saint and sinner. They experienced the human drama in all its heights and depths, joys and sorrows. Those who learned to trust in God and to see their difficulties through His perspective came through each experience stronger than they were before. Just as God was with His people of old who struggled, He is also with us as we invite Him into our situations.

To help us gain God's perspective on adversity, we're going to look at two accounts of biblical characters who had to learn to trust in God in the midst of their troubles. These are stories of real people, with real problems. The first story is about a woman whose life and spiritual growth show us a crucial aspect of God's perspective: He is more interested in changing *us* than in changing our circumstances, because the real victory over adversity occurs within our own hearts. The second story is about a man whose difficulties reveal God's highest priority during our trials: deepening our relationship with Him.

Leah's Story:
The Change Is Within

Leah Was in a Situation beyond Her Control

Leah was suffering in the midst of a circumstance that was totally beyond her control. To understand the real plight

127

of her situation, we must go back and examine the beginning of her dilemma. This story could rival the plots of any of today's soap operas.

Leah was married to a man named Jacob. Her husband was the son of Isaac and the grandson of Abraham. Jacob had a twin brother named Esau. Because Esau was the firstborn, he was entitled to the family birthright. However, Jacob tricked his brother, cheating him out of his birthright. Esau became enraged, and Jacob had to run for his life. He traveled more than four hundred miles to a place called Haran, where Laban—his mother Rebekah's brother—lived. Jacob intended to stay there until Esau's anger subsided. He also intended to find a wife there from among his mother's relatives.

When Jacob arrived in Haran, he stopped at a well that was used for watering sheep. Laban's daughter Rachel, who was *"beautiful of form and appearance"* (Genesis 29:17), came to water Laban's flock, and when Jacob saw her, the Bible says he was so enthralled with her that he was overcome with emotion. *"Jacob kissed Rachel, and lifted up his voice and wept"* (v. 11). Jacob told Rachel that he was Laban's nephew, and she ran to tell her father.

When Laban heard the news of Jacob's arrival, he went out to meet him, embraced him, and brought him to his house. He then offered him a place to stay and a job. When Jacob agreed, Laban asked him what he thought would be a fair wage. Jacob told him that he would work for him for seven years, and in place of wages, he wanted Laban's permission to marry Rachel. It was the custom of the day for a man to present a dowry or a "bride price" to the family of his future wife. This was to compensate the family for the loss of their daughter and the free labor that she provided. Since Jacob had no material possessions, he offered to work for Rachel's hand in marriage instead. Laban agreed. However, he did not tell Jacob of another custom of the land: an older daughter in the family had to be married before a younger daughter could be married.

Leah was Rachel's older sister. The Bible tells us that Rachel was beautiful but that Leah's eyes were *"delicate"* (v. 17). The word for *"delicate"* in the Hebrew is *rak*. One translation for this word is "weak." Some say this means that

Leah was weak-eyed or timid or that she had no "sparkle." Others translate *rak* as "tender-eyed," saying that Leah had attractive, "dreamy" eyes. However, the key to the true meaning of *rak* lies in a small word in verse seventeen: *"Leah's eyes were delicate, **but** Rachel was beautiful of form and appearance"* (emphasis added). In other words, whatever Rachel was, Leah was not.

Verse eighteen says, *"Jacob loved Rachel."* We could translate this as, "Jacob greatly favored Rachel." He didn't know her well enough yet to love her. Rather, he was attracted to her tremendous physical beauty. Jacob favored Rachel over Leah.

After the seven years were completed, Laban held the wedding feast. When the festivities were over and it was late at night, Laban sent Leah, instead of Rachel, in to Jacob. Jacob was not aware of the switch until the morning. You may wonder how he could have been so easily deceived. However, in ancient times, a bride was very heavily veiled during a wedding feast, and the bedchamber was

LEAH WAS UNLOVED.

kept very dark "for atmosphere." Between the darkness, the veils, the lateness of the hour, and Jacob perhaps having consumed a great deal of wine at the feast, we can see how he was deceived.

Laban knew how much Jacob wanted Rachel. He knew that Jacob would do just about anything to have her. Therefore, when Jacob confronted Laban about the deception, Laban agreed to give him Rachel as a wife also—in exchange for an additional seven years' work. Within about a two-week period, Jacob received two wives for a bride price of fourteen years' work.

The Bible tells us that Jacob *"loved Rachel more than Leah"* (Genesis 29:30); therefore, *"Leah was unloved"* (v. 31). Leah had to live with the fact that Jacob and Rachel had a special love for each another. She had to confront her misery every single day. Imagine Leah walking by her sister's tent at night and listening to Rachel's and Jacob's laughter. Picture her sitting at every meal as Rachel and Jacob gazed into each other's eyes. Perhaps worst of all, Leah knew that when she was with her husband, his mind was on his *other* wife.

Leah's Situation Did Not Change

Leah had a miserable life. She was in a permanent situation that was totally beyond her control. She couldn't help the fact that she was not as beautiful as her sister. Moreover, she had been forced into her father's deceptive scheme. There are some situations in life that we just cannot change.

Yet God was working in the midst of Leah's bitter circumstances. He saw her misery, and in His mercy, He *"opened her womb"* (v. 31). While Rachel was barren, Leah conceived and bore a son. She called him Reuben, which means something like, "See—a son!" Leah thought her troubles might be over. *"The LORD has surely looked on my affliction. Now therefore, my husband will love me"* (Genesis 29:32), she said.

However, Leah's situation did not change, even after she conceived again and bore a second son, Simeon. Leah said, *"Because the LORD has heard that I am unloved, He has therefore given me this son also"* (v. 33). But things stayed the same. Then she bore a third son, whom she named Levi, which means "attached." After Levi was born, she said, *"Now this time my husband will become attached to me, because I have borne him three sons"* (v. 34).

Something Changed within Leah

Leah was suffering immense loneliness and heartbreak through no fault of her own, and she was searching for a solution to her dilemma. She thought bearing children might bring her favor with Jacob. Yet Leah's situation did not change even after she bore Jacob three sons.

The Bible reveals that something *did* change however—something changed *within Leah*. When she conceived and bore a fourth son, she called him Judah, which means "praised" or "celebrated," and she declared, *"Now I will praise the LORD"* (v. 35). Leah named her baby "praise." Her other sons were given names that reflected her desperation, fear, and discontent. When we are in a state of dissatisfaction, we can conceive and give birth to depression and anxiety. Then we feed and nurture them, and they grow in our lives. Fear and worry become our offspring, just as the names of Leah's first three sons represented her fear and worry.

Yet Leah named her new baby "praise," as if to say, "Lord, I don't recognize what You are doing, but I praise You anyway. *This time*, I will praise the Lord." Leah still longed for the love of her husband, and she still entered into rivalry with her sister when the circumstances of her life got the better of her and she reacted with anger. However, Leah experienced a major breakthrough at the time of Judah's birth. She switched her focus from her difficulty to God, and she praised Him for His continual faithfulness.

Leah Was Honored by God and by Her Husband

What was the outcome of Leah's life? Rachel eventually had two children, Joseph and Benjamin, but Leah had seven children: Reuben, Simeon, Levi, Judah, Issachar, Zebulun, and Dinah. Her fourth son, Judah, the "praise child," was the son through whom the tribe of Judah came. That means that, through her bloodline, King David and the long-awaited Messiah were born.

The woman who was "unloved" was immensely blessed by God to be an ancestor of the Lord Jesus Christ. Yet there is something else in Leah's life that is fascinating. In Genesis 23, Abraham had purchased the cave of Machpelah as a family burial place. Abraham was buried there, along with his wife Sarah. Isaac and Rebekah were also buried there. We learn that when Rachel died in childbirth, Jacob buried

YOU DON'T KNOW THE GOOD THINGS GOD HAS PLANNED.

her on the road to Bethlehem and set up a pillar on her grave (Genesis 35:16–20). When Leah died, however, Jacob buried her in the family burial place. When Jacob was dying, he asked his sons to bury him there also (Genesis 49:29–33). Leah was given a place of family honor by being buried with Jacob.

It is not entirely clear why Jacob buried Leah rather than Rachel at Machpelah. Perhaps Jacob had learned to appreciate qualities in Leah that he had previously overlooked. Whatever the reason, Rachel was left buried by the side of the road, while Leah—the ancestor of the Messiah— was buried in the family grave along with the patriarchs Abraham, Isaac, and Jacob.

Some Things Are Not Meant to Be Changed

You don't know what God has planned for you in your suffering. The longer I live on this earth, the more I understand what Paul meant when he said, *"Tribulation produces perseverance; and perseverance, character; and character, hope"* (Romans 5:3–4). I am not certain of the origin of the theology that says, "If you just pray hard enough and long enough, everything will change the way you want it to." This idea is not scriptural. There are some things we are not meant to change. There are some things we are meant only to survive and outlive. *Every* person you pray for who has a life-threatening disease or injury may not live—no matter how much you fast and pray. *Every* broken relationship that you ask God to restore may not be restored.

At times God does work in miraculous ways to save and deliver His people. He heals, restores, and changes circumstances. Yet, again, some things are not meant to be changed. When you encounter such instances, you need to keep the following truth in mind: You are to claim the victory of Christ over *all* things, for *all eternity.* However, you may still have to suffer for a time on this earth. When you do, God will use your suffering to develop His nature and character in you. If God answered every one of your prayers, according to your will, you would never have to endure anything. If you never have to endure anything, you will lack wisdom in the things of God and will not develop the character of Christ, who endured much for your sake: *"For the joy that was set before Him* [Jesus] *endured the cross"* (Hebrews 12:2).

The Change Is Within

God did not change Leah's situation, but He changed her attitude toward her situation so that she could praise Him in the midst of it. As believers, we must remember that we live on a sinful earth and that we are affected by the results of sin and evil. We should ask God to help us to endure the effects of evil and to remove our anger and bitterness over our circumstances by changing our attitudes.

We do not pray to God only to get Him to do what we want Him to do. The purpose of prayer is to give us an opportunity to get close to God. You cannot become close to somebody whom you don't talk to on a regular basis. Some of the unchangeable circumstances in your life are put there by God to develop your prayer life and your character, and to increase your level of endurance. It is essential for you to remember Paul's words in Romans 5:3–5:

➤ *Tribulation* produces perseverance.
➤ *Perseverance* produces character.
➤ *Character* produces hope.
➤ *Hope* does not disappoint us.

The very things that are difficult for you, the things you want to change, the things you want to escape—are the very things that will make you strong. What is

immovable,
unchangeable,
inflexible,
fixed,
rigid

in your life will cause your spirit to rise up and tell the devil, "*This time, I will praise the Lord.* You tormented my mind, troubled my heart, dashed my hopes, and stole my joy, but *this time, I'm going to give birth to praise.*" You can tell God, "I don't quite understand the reason why You are allowing these things to occur in my life, and quite frankly, I don't like what is happening to me, but this time, I will praise You regardless of my circumstances."

Leah named her baby "praise." She learned to take her eyes off her circumstances and to focus on God. She could have continued feeling sorry for herself, being depressed and wallowing in self-pity. However, she pulled herself together and said, *"This time, I will praise the Lord."* Your spiritual prognosis will be excellent when you can praise the Lord in the midst of your trials, and when you realize that God is more interested in changing you than in changing your immediate circumstances. His greatest desire is that you will develop the character and mind· of Christ.

John the Baptist's Story:
Relationship rather than Deliverance

John the Baptist is another biblical character whose life reveals important truths about God's perspective on our suffering and how we can maintain a good spiritual prognosis in the midst of our trials. His story shows us that our own sufferings have more to do with our relationship with God than with deliverance from our trials.

It Wasn't Supposed to Be like This

What was the single most deciding factor that caused you to turn away from a life of sin and make a decision to live for Christ? Allow me to offer the following answer to the question, because I have heard this answer given hundreds of times from people who have walked boldly down the aisle of the church and publicly given their hearts to Jesus. No matter what sins they were turning away from, no matter what their circumstances, when I asked them the question I posed above, their answers were almost always the same: "I just got tired. I got tired of what I was doing and how I was living. I wanted a change in my life, so I decided to try Jesus." That is a valid reason for coming to God. Whatever motivated, stirred, or influenced you to make a decision for Christ was valid if your heart was sincere and you meant what you told God about turning your life over to Him.

THE CHRISTIAN LIFE DOES NOT GUARANTEE A PROBLEM-FREE EXISTENCE.

Yet turning our lives over to God is only the beginning of our walk with Him. Many times, when people make the decision to follow Christ and they enter into the new life He gives, they find out that being a Christian is not what they thought it would be. They believed it would be an "escape route" from all their pain, problems, and heartaches. They thought they would be living a life of comfort and ease, where they would no longer have any cares or concerns.

The Christian life *does* bring us tremendous peace and joy because our sins are forgiven and our relationship with

God is restored. The Bible says that the *"kingdom of God is...righteousness and peace and joy in the Holy Spirit"* (Romans 14:17). Many new Christians experience this peace and joy when they first come to Christ. Yet often they do not understand that the Christian life is not carefree, and when the first sign of trouble comes, they react with bewilderment and shock. They do not realize (1) that they still live in a fallen world, and (2) that the Christian life has its own set of tests and trials, stresses and heartaches. These afflictions can often make us feel as if there is a heavy burden upon us. Many Christians, if they did not know better, might say that it is easier to remain in the world than to be a follower of Christ. However, that is a shortsighted perspective on what life in Christ really means.

John's Suffering Made Him Begin to Doubt His Calling

When Jesus was teaching the multitudes, He talked about the heavy burdens we bear in life (Matthew 11:28–30). John the Baptist—who had been called by God from birth to prepare the Hebrew people for the ministry of Jesus—was in prison at this time, bearing his own burden. John had been imprisoned by Herod because he had told Herod it was not lawful for him to have his brother's wife. While John was in jail, he heard about all the miracles Jesus was doing, and so he sent two of his own disciples to Jesus in order to ask Him a crucial question: *"Are You the Coming One, or do we look for another?"* (Matthew 11:3). John wanted to know, "Are You really the Messiah, or should I keep on looking for Him?"

This seems like a strange question coming from the man whom the prophet Isaiah called *"the voice of one crying in the wilderness: 'Prepare the way of the LORD'"* (Isaiah 40:3). His whole life had been devoted to the coming of the Messiah. His birth had been prophesied several thousand years before he was born, and the angel who announced his birth to his parents Elizabeth and Zacharias made it clear that he would be set apart for God's service. John had a specific role to play in God's plan for the world. His job was to point people to Jesus, and he put all his energies into that task.

However, when John ended up in prison, he began to have some doubts about whether Jesus was really the Messiah. He must have been thinking something like, "If my

135

purpose is to prepare people for the coming Messiah, and if Jesus of Nazareth is that Messiah, then why am I in prison suffering and going through such a difficult trial? I should be out preaching to the crowds, continuing to prepare their hearts to receive the Savior."

Jesus answered John's doubts about His Messiahship by pointing to His acts of healing the blind, the lame, the deaf, and the lepers; casting out demons and raising the dead; and preaching the Good News about God's plan of redemption. He pointed to the fulfillment of all the things that had been prophesied about Him. With so much evidence, there was no mistaking Jesus' identity.

John's Obedience Brought Him Suffering and Martyrdom

Jesus then gave John a tremendous compliment and show of support by saying, *"Assuredly, I say to you, among those born of women there has not risen one greater than John the Baptist"* (Matthew 11:11). Jesus was referring to John's level of obedience and commitment to God. John was fulfilling his calling, his God-given purpose for his life. Yet there he was—cold, hungry, and shackled in prison. John was being obedient to God, and his obedience had landed him in jail. Instead of being rewarded, he seemed only to be given great suffering.

It is noteworthy that in the midst of all the good things that Jesus said about John, Jesus never spoke about miraculously delivering John from prison or bringing an end to his suffering. Jesus was the Miracle Worker. He could have summoned angels to release John from prison. He could have waved His hand and caused an earthquake to shake loose the prison bars. He could have destroyed John's accusers. John was probably wondering why Jesus seemed to be doing nothing to secure his release. Instead, Jesus just continued teaching and preaching to the people—and John ended up dying in prison.

Rest from Trials Comes from Being Yoked with Christ

In Matthew 14, we learn that John was beheaded by Herod. His head was placed on a serving tray at the ruler's birthday party and presented to the daughter of Herod's unlawful wife. John died a cruel and senseless death. Yet Jesus never intervened for John in his suffering. He did not prevent John's agony and anguish. Instead, His response to John's situation was to give a remarkable open invitation to all people:

Come to Me, all you who labor and are heavy laden, and I will give you rest. Take My yoke upon you and learn from Me, for I am gentle and lowly in heart, and you will find rest for your souls. For My yoke is easy and My burden is light. (Matthew 11:28–30)

This response was also Christ's answer to John the Baptist's perplexity about his trial. Jesus was saying, "All of you who

suffer,
are burdened,
are going through trials,
labor beneath any type of yoke,

I invite you to come to Me and put on My yoke. It is light; therefore, it is easy to bear. Allow Me to teach and train you, for My teachings are gentle and humble, and as you receive them, you will find rest for your souls." A yoke is a wooden frame placed over the heads of two animals, such as oxen, to make them work together. Jesus invites us to be yoked with Him so that we will be working to-

JESUS DID NOT PREVENT JOHN'S SUFFERING.

ward the same purposes and in the same manner. With His person and power beside us, we can endure every difficult circumstance. In this way, we find true strength and rest in Him.

Jesus did *not* say, "I invite you to come to Me so that I can give you an escape from your problems, a way out of your difficulties, freedom from hardship, and detachment from the realities of life." He said He would give us *rest for our souls.* John the Baptist fulfilled the purpose to which God had called him; this purpose included persecution and suffering as a prophet of God. His life was a demonstration that while God offers all people salvation and rest, not everyone will choose to forsake the burdens of sin and evil and find peace in God. Those who reject God's offer will end up working on satan's behalf and attacking God's people. Yet for those who belong to Christ, such persecution comes with great blessing. Jesus said to His disciples,

> *Blessed are those who are persecuted for righteousness' sake, for theirs is the kingdom of heaven. Blessed are you when they revile and persecute you, and say all kinds of evil against you falsely for My sake. Rejoice and be exceedingly glad, for great is your reward in heaven, for so they persecuted the prophets who were before you.* (Matthew 5:10–12)

John the Baptist was one of those persecuted prophets, and His reward in heaven will be great. The sufferings he experienced in this life will seem small in comparison to the blessings of eternity. He can now say, as did the apostle Paul, *"For our light affliction, which is but for a moment, is working for us a far more exceeding and eternal weight of glory"* (2 Corinthians 4:17).

Jesus' Rest Means Intimate Relationship with God

The rest that Jesus offers is like no other rest. It does not mean freedom from labor. It means entering into *an intimate, loving relationship with God* through Jesus Christ. Our intimacy with God is represented by "taking on the yoke" of Christ as we walk and work side by side with Him. The yoke that Christ gives makes us stronger and develops qualities in us that will help us to live better in the present and to prepare for our future. It can transform worrisome toil into spiritual productivity and purpose. That was the yoke, and that was the rest, that John received.

When Jesus says, *"Come to Me"* (Matthew 11:28), He is giving us an open invitation overflowing with opportunity. Christ is calling us to *Himself.* *"'Come to Me, all you who labor and are heavy laden'* (v. 28). All who are tired, weary, and worn out with life, and who feel like giving up—*'Come to Me...and I will give you rest'* (v. 28)."

Jesus does not necessarily mean that we will be given

escape,

a way out,

freedom from pain,

but that we will be given His *rest*—a deep sense of spiritual well-being and supernatural strength for living. Jesus gives us rest so that we can recover, recuperate, learn, understand, and grow as a result of our troubles.

"Take My yoke upon you" (v. 29). When a yoke is placed upon an animal's back, it indicates that there is work to be done and that the work will be tedious and burdensome. But while our trials can often feel like burdens, this is not what Christ intends by His statement, *"Take My yoke upon you."* There is an additional meaning to the word *yoke* besides shouldering a burden. It can mean "an obligation or a responsibility." Jesus says, *"'Take My yoke upon you and learn from Me'* (v. 29). Take the responsibility to learn about who I am, and let Me teach, instruct, and train you in My ways." We are to increase our knowledge of Christ, not only so that we may know His teachings, but also so that we can apply that knowledge to our lives through a living relationship with Him. As a result, we will be able to walk with new strength, function with new effectiveness, and live with new vitality.

WE ARE YOKED WITH CHRIST TO FULFILL GOD'S PURPOSES.

When Christ invites us to take His yoke, it may sometimes seem as if He is saying, "Let me replace one set of burdens with another." That is not the case. He replaces our weakness with His strength, so that we will be able to bear the burden of life's tribulations, while building spiritual strength and stamina at the same time. Jesus said, *"In the world you will have tribulation; but be of good cheer, I have overcome the world"* (John 16:33). Because He overcame, we can overcome, too. In the midst of our trials, He will give us rest, recuperation, and recovery for our souls. That is God's promise to us.

God has yoked us together with Christ so that we may effectively work together with our Lord to further His kingdom and fulfill our role in it. We are not left alone; we are not left to stumble around in the dark. When we take upon ourselves the obligation and the responsibility to learn from Jesus, Jesus tells us He will put Himself under the yoke with us. With Christ, we can bear the burden and carry the load. This is not a yoke that Christ gives us, but one that He *shares* with us, so that we will have balance. We do not fulfill our calling alone. The Spirit of Christ works with us.

Remember that Christ's strength is made perfect in our weaknesses (2 Corinthians 12:9). When the Egyptians tried to wear down the Hebrew people by forcing them into slavery and mistreating them, the pain and hardship of slavery only caused the Hebrews to multiply and grow stronger instead. Our burdens are not to make us *bitter;* they are to make us *better.* Even the worst situations can make us better people. We cannot be overcomers if we have nothing to overcome. Sometimes life can be like a heavy yoke, but *"all things work together for good to those who love God, to those who are the called according to His purpose"* (Romans 8:28). Christ replaces our heavy yokes with His light yoke—the yoke of an intimate relationship with Him that brings us love and joy in the Holy Spirit. Christ's yoke will not overload us or weigh us down. Wearing the yoke of Christ will require commitment, sacrifice, consistency, and patience, just as it did for John the Baptist. However, it will bring us blessing, power, strength, assurance, hope, wisdom, and faith.

As you read the accounts of other biblical characters, you can glean many more truths that will give you God's perspective on your adversities. Just as God was with people of old who struggled, He is also with us as we invite Him into our situations. When you read the Word of God, ask the Holy Spirit, your Attending Physician, to show you lessons, commands, solutions, remedies, and examples from the lives of God's people that you can apply as *strong medicine* to your life situations.

GOD'S PROVISIONS

Regardless of how mighty we may be in God, all of us have times when we are spiritually depleted and need to be replenished. God anticipated these times, and He has made provision for our spiritual well-being in the midst of our trials and spiritual "dry spells." At the beginning of this chapter, I said that the doctors kept me in a step-down unit when I was recovering from meningitis because they wanted to make sure that my condition was stable. My good prognosis depended not only upon the initial critical care I received but also upon the follow-up care I had while I was in the hospital and when I went home to continue my recuperation. Likewise, God's provision for your spiritual well-being ensures that your spiritual condition during trials will remain "stable" and that your follow-up care will advance your spiritual growth.

Two crucial areas can cause us setbacks in the midst of our trials, but God has given us *strong medicine* to address these issues so that we can maintain an excellent spiritual prognosis. These areas are (1) fear and despair; (2) living in the past.

Fear and Despair

Even if you are strong in the Lord today, if you don't maintain the consistent, intimate relationship with the Lord that comes from being yoked with Christ, then fear and despair can overwhelm you, weakening your spiritual prognosis. Sometimes, when we do not receive the quick fix for our difficulties that we expected, an overwhelming sense of fear paralyzes us because we feel totally helpless. Fear is a dark shadow that blocks the truth of God's Word and ultimately imprisons us within ourselves. Each of us has been a prisoner of fear at one time or another. We have been imprisoned by the fear of unanswered questions, misunderstanding, uncertainty, sickness, death, or "the fear of fear itself." But fear can be conquered by the bright, liberating light of the Lord, who is our Salvation. If you want to dispel the darkness of fear in your life, remember the words of David, *"The LORD is my light and my salvation; whom shall I fear? The LORD is the strength of my life; of whom shall I be afraid?"* (Psalm 27:1). When you trust in the light and strength of the Lord to lead and sustain you, you will be able to conquer fear in your life.

"The LORD is my light and my salvation; whom shall I fear?" God's light enables us to replace our fears with a constructive response to our difficulties. It gives us the ability to see beyond our circumstances and into God's purposes for us in the midst of them. I laugh now at some experiences that at the time brought tears to my eyes and much anguish to my heart. My greatest joy is that in all my trials I was always able to pause in the midst of my emotions to ask the question, "What can I learn from this experience?" Then, as I received God's answer to this question, I was able to learn what He wanted to teach me through my situation and apply it to my life.

Our best lessons are learned through our problems. A problem is not really a roadblock; it is more like a "yield" sign that gives us time to slow down and ask ourselves important questions. Somewhere deep inside us, we know that we are being allowed to experience difficult times in order to learn something about ourselves or God. Perhaps we have experienced a similar situation in the past but have not tried to find out what we could learn from it. Sometimes similar problems reoccur in our lives until we discover and learn the lessons we are meant to learn—lessons that are critical to our spiritual well-being. Experiencing pain is unavoidable. We cannot live life without undergoing its inevitable upheavals. But *persistent* suffering is something we sometimes "choose"—simply by choosing not to do anything constructive about it.

"The LORD is the strength of my life; of whom shall I be afraid?" God provides us with strength as well as light in the midst of our trials. We often feel afraid because we are helpless and powerless to change our situations. At these times, we need to remember that we are to rely on God's strength rather than our own abilities. We are not equal to the challenges or uncertainties we are facing, but we do not have to fear, because God is more than equal to them. We can receive His strength so that, no matter what happens, we will be able to respond with steadiness and faith.

It can be extremely difficult to shake off feelings of fear. However, when we truly know that we can put our anxiety in God's hands and receive His light and strength to endure our circumstances, then we will be able to overcome our fears.

This is important because the lessons we learn from our adversities are not just for our own use. Whenever I learn a new life lesson from a trial, I store it in the cupboard of my memory so that I can later take it out and pass it along to others in need. In this way, my fear is transformed into grace and healing for both myself and others.

At times we will all feel anxious, frightened, fragile, and out of control. Our challenge is not to despair, but to keep moving forward despite setbacks and fears. We cannot allow our moods and impulses to control our responses to our trials, or our spiritual growth will be hindered. Whenever you feel afraid, practice keeping your mind focused on the Lord and His love rather than on your difficulty, and repeat this verse to yourself: *"He will keep in perfect peace all those who trust in him, whose thoughts turn often to the Lord! Trust in the Lord God always, for in the Lord Jehovah is your everlasting strength* (Isaiah 26:3–4 TLB). Trusting in God is the antidote to fear.

TRUST IS THE ANTIDOTE TO FEAR.

Living in the Past

Despite the fact that many of us know all the Bible verses about forgiveness and mercy, some of us still operate under a tremendous cloud of "If I just hadn't done that." As a result, we do not allow ourselves to be totally yielded and committed to God, and we find ourselves in a place of stagnation and inactivity. We are unable to progress in our life in Christ. Some believers are not able to move forward and grow in God because of an overwhelming sense of shame and remorse about situations and circumstances over which they did not have any control or that happened years ago. Satan will always attempt to cause you to be preoccupied with your past. He will harass you about what you used to do and how you used to live until you are filled with regret and sorrow. Then you are not free to move forward in the freedom that comes with knowing, *"If the Son makes you free, you shall be free indeed"* (John 8:36).

I want to emphasize that there is a big difference between reviewing our past experiences so that we may learn and grow from them, and dwelling on our experiences to the point that we become paralyzed with guilt and fear. God uses the former to make us spiritually strong, but the devil uses the latter to weaken us in the things of God.

Paul was a great apostle and one of the most prolific writers of the New Testament. Yet, more than anyone, he had reason to feel guilty. Before he accepted Christ, he put all of his efforts and energy into persecuting Christians. He hunted them down like dogs. At one point, he received special permission to travel to various towns on a mission to find Christians and destroy their lives. He even held the coats of those who stoned Stephen. So Paul had many reasons to feel guilty. But in one of his letters of encouragement to the church at Philippi, he wrote,

> *Brethren, I do not count myself to have apprehended* [perfection in Christ]; *but one thing I do, forgetting those things which are behind and reaching forward to those things which are ahead, I press toward the goal for the prize of the upward call of God in Christ Jesus.* (Philippians 3:13–14)

Paul was saying, in essence, "I am still not all that I should be, but I am bringing all of my energies to bear on this one thing: I am forgetting the past and looking forward to what lies ahead. I am straining to do my best and to reach the end of the race. I am doing this so that I may receive the prize for which God is calling us all to heaven because of what Christ Jesus did for us."

Paul wrote in Romans 3:23, *"For all have sinned and fall short of the glory of God."* The word *"all"* is totally inclusive. Sometimes we make the mistake of comparing our sins with the sins of others, thinking, "I am not as bad as he is" or, "Compared to her, I'm not a very good Christian." We must understand that God does not see sin in degrees. Hatred and gossip are as sinful as murder, lying, and lust. Any sin we commit makes us a sinner because sin—regardless of what form it takes—cuts us off from God. Being cut off from God, who is the only Giver of life, leads to death.

Yet the good news of the Bible is this: there is a way to be declared "not guilty" for our sins. When a judge in a court of law declares a defendant "not guilty," all the charges are removed from the defendant's record. Legally, it is as if the person had never been accused of that particular crime. Similarly, when God forgives your sins, your record is wiped clean. It is not covered up or hidden away, only to be pulled out at a later time and thrown in your face. Instead, it is *wiped clean.* It is as if God took a big eraser and rubbed away every sinful act, every bad decision, every wrong choice, every foolish mistake, and every unwise action you ever made. The blood of Jesus Christ wiped your sins away. When you repented, confessed your sins, and put your trust and confidence in the finished work of Jesus Christ—which effected your forgiveness—you were made right with God.

Every one of us, no matter who we are and what we are like, can be declared "not guilty" in this way. Our acquittal is not based upon our good deeds or who we know. We have been set free from the penalty of sin purely because of God's love for us and Christ's sacrificial death on our behalf.

Paul said that, after you have been acquitted—after you have been declared not guilty—if you allow yourself to feel condemned about what you used to do and how you used to live, you do not understand that Christ freed you not only from the *penalty* of sin, but also from the *condemnation* of sin. *"There is therefore now no condemnation to those who are in Christ Jesus, who do not walk according to the flesh, but according to the Spirit"* (Romans 8:1).

What would the words *"there is therefore now no condemnation"* mean to you if you were on death row? You would no longer have to fear execution. The fact is that the whole human race is on death row. Yet because of Christ's death on the cross, we are not only free from sin, but also free to live our lives without guilt or fear of God's punishment for things for which we already have been forgiven. Yes, we deserve punishment for our sins. But Christ has taken our punishment upon Himself, so that we no longer have to experience it.

YOU HAVE BEEN DECLARED "NOT GUILTY."

Nowhere in Scripture are you told that you have to first "get right" or "clean up your act" before you can come to

Christ. Jesus says, "Come just as you are." God's Word is clear. If you desire to repent and turn from your sins, only two things are required for you to come to Christ, and they are found in Romans 10:9:

Rx Confess with your mouth that Jesus is Lord.
Rx Believe in your heart that God raised Jesus from the dead.

If you do these two things, *"you will be saved"* (v. 9). *"Saved"* from what? The penalty of sin. God's message is plain and simple. If God has no other qualification for salvation, then why should we create one by trying to "pay" for our sins with our guilt? Paul said that he had not yet attained perfection in Christ. None of us has. We all have done things we wish we had not done. We live in the tension of what we used to be and what we want to be. Yet because of our hope in Christ, we can let go of the guilt of the past and look forward to what we will become as we yield ourselves to Christ.

You must keep in mind that the devil's objective is to prevent you from realizing your potential in God. There may be certain areas in your life where you are still struggling. There may be areas in your life where you thought you had the victory, but then yielded to temptation. Satan will remind you of these things until you start believing you were never really saved. However, even when you fail, *"there is therefore now no condemnation to those who are in Christ Jesus"* (Romans 8:1). When we fail, we can go to God and ask His forgiveness based on the blood of Christ that was shed for us.

There is a popular slogan that says, "Please be patient with me. God is not finished with me yet." However, some Christians are uncomfortable with the idea that, on a daily basis, they may be talking with, worshipping with, serving with, and fellowshipping with people who are still struggling with serious life issues, such as addiction. People who have committed their lives to Christ but are trying to overcome their problems are often just as uncomfortable, because they fear that, because they are still struggling with certain issues, perhaps they have not been forgiven for their sin after all. We must understand that, even as we struggle with lingering sin in our lives, what we were in the past is not what we are now, if we have truly committed our lives to Christ. God is in the process of transforming us into the image of His Son. We have to be patient with ourselves—and others— in the midst of this process.

God erased all of your sin when He saved you. He sees the potential of what you can be if you keep your heart, your mind, and your spirit focused upon Him. God sees you as one who is spiritually prosperous and redeemed, blessed and born again, saved and forgiven, transformed and heaven bound. This is the image you are to have of yourself in the midst of your trials and whenever you start to feel guilty for sins that have already been forgiven. Resting in Christ's forgiveness and trusting in His power to transform you is God's *strong medicine* that will enable you to maintain a good prognosis as you move forward in your spiritual development.

GOD'S PLAN

When I was in the hospital, the point of all the specialized care I received, and the doctors' diagnosis, prognosis, and treatment of my condition, was to help me progress in healing so that I could return to normal health. Spiritual healing is even better than physical healing in that we not only regain our former spiritual strength, which may have been weakened during the crisis or trial we experienced, but also gain additional spiritual benefits. Our spiritual growth during adversity is exponential.

It is important to keep in mind that how we grow and what we learn from our life experiences are often greater than the experiences themselves, because what we take away from them is much more valuable to us. That is why Paul was able to say,

> For our light affliction, which is but for a moment, is working for us a far more exceeding and eternal weight of glory, while we do not look at the things which are seen, but at the things which are not seen. For the things which are seen are temporary, but the things which are not seen are eternal.
> (2 Corinthians 4:17–18)

147

If we gain strength, wisdom, and compassion from having gone through a very difficult experience, then we are taking away something very valuable from it that we might never have gained in any other way. Moreover, what we gain, we will keep for all eternity. There are some circumstances in life that may always cause us sadness when we think about them, but when our hurt has begun to heal and we are able to learn what God wants to teach us from these circumstances, then what we gain will be of great spiritual value to us. The negative experience, like many of our memories, may fade, but what is lasting—a deeper relationship with God, spiritual strength, wisdom, and compassion for others—will always remain with us.

I wrote in chapter one of this book that my illness changed the trajectory of my life. My experience was not just a physical illness where I had to be cured using medication and hospitalization. This was a circumstance that God allowed in my life in order to show me something greater about Himself and to prepare me to go to the next level of spiritual maturity. Although I was growing in the Lord, depending on Him, and serving Him before my illness, this experience took me to a new level in my relationship with God, enabling me to focus on Him and to depend on Him as never before. I saw His power manifested in my weakness, accomplishing what I never could have accomplished on my own. My relationship with the Lord and my ministry are now fuller, richer, and deeper than they would have been had I not undergone this trial. I have seen a similar process repeated in the lives of many other believers. God's plan for our growth in spiritual maturity is to move us from level to level in our understanding and commitment to Him, so that we will continually *"grow in the grace and knowledge of our Lord and Savior Jesus Christ"* (2 Peter 3:18). Sometimes it takes a powerful life experience to take us to the next spiritual level.

GOD MOVES US TO GREATER LEVELS OF SPIRITUAL MATURITY.

The prospect or possibility of one's own untimely death is probably the most frightening situation that a person can face. My experience in the emergency room was so strong and devastating that since I recovered, every other difficult situation I have experienced in life has paled in comparison. At the time, I felt that if I could face serious illness and death, and come through it, then I would always have that crisis as a point of reference for anything the enemy might present to me or use against me in my life. Knowing how the power of God can work when my faith meets His strength has armed me to confront any other challenge that the enemy might send my way. Facing death was the final hill to climb, the last big hurdle for me to cross, to strengthen my faith to the level at which I could be most effective in the ministry to which God has called me.

For every level of spiritual growth, God takes us to a deeper depth and a greater height of faith and grace, much like going up stair steps. During my recovery from my illness, and when I was finally restored to full health, I realized that the purpose of my illness was so that I could move to the next level of faith, strength, and stability, and into an even deeper, more intimate relationship with God. Without this growth, I would not be able to fulfill the tremendous vision for ministry that God had assigned to my life. The spiritual strength that I had for the previous level was good for where I was at that point. But I had to be prepared for the larger-than-life vision God had given me, not only so that I could be spiritually mature enough to carry out the vision, but also so that I could handle whatever difficulties the enemy might use to try to make me afraid of the vision— thereby causing me to hold back on it or to abandon it entirely.

Progressing through levels of faith is like receiving a vaccination. Vaccinations are designed to introduce a disease into your body in a very small amount, so that you will build up antibodies to it. In this way, when you encounter the actual disease, it won't affect you because you will have built up a resistance to it. When God brings us through levels of faith, the first trial we encounter often isn't going to be as difficult as subsequent trials. His hedge of protection is usually taken away gradually, because we are not strong enough at first to deal with more difficult problems. *"God is faithful, who will not allow you to be tempted beyond what you are able"* (1 Corinthians 10:13). Similar to a vaccination, when

God allows us to go through increasingly challenging times, He is building up our "faith resistance."

We will all have many corners to turn in life, many difficulties to overcome. However, most of us will have one major event in life that will catapult us to a faith level where we are able to believe God for *anything* because of what we've gone through and because we have come through the experience victoriously. That is not to say that after such an experience we will no longer need to progress to new levels in our spiritual growth. Rather, it means that we will always be able to refer to that experience in all our future difficulties and adversities. In this way, we will be able to rely on the strength God has given us and the testimony of past victory to see us through whatever else comes our way.

I invite you to pray this prayer so that you will maintain an excellent spiritual prognosis:

> *Lord, You know what I am going through, and You know the diagnosis of my situation. I ask You to keep me close to You as I work through all that You want to teach me through my adversity. I pray that You will enable me to maintain an excellent spiritual prognosis by helping me to keep in mind Your promises to me as Your child, Your perspective on my adversity, Your provision for my spiritual well-being, and Your plan for my spiritual growth. Let me grow in faith and grace so that I can progress to the next level of spiritual maturity in You. In Jesus' name, I pray. Amen.*

Spiritual Vitamins

☐ Set aside some time this week to look at your difficulty in light of the spiritual provisions God has made for you through His presence in your life and the power of His Word to transform you.

☐ For the next week, pray the prayer at the end of chapter five, so that you can focus on maintaining a strong spiritual prognosis.

☐ Read and memorize these verses, so that you will remember to look at your difficulty in light of who God is rather than in the shadow of your own weakness:

The righteous cry out, and the LORD hears, and delivers them out of all their troubles. The LORD is near to those who have a broken heart, and saves such as have a contrite spirit. Many are the afflictions of the righteous, but the LORD delivers him out of them all.
(Psalm 34:17–19)

Trust in the LORD with all your heart, and lean not on your own understanding; in all your ways acknowledge Him, and He shall direct your paths.
(Proverbs 3:5–6)

We also glory in tribulations, knowing that tribulation produces perseverance; and perseverance, character; and character, hope. Now hope does not disappoint, because the love of God has been poured out in our hearts by the Holy Spirit who was given to us.
(Romans 5:3–5)

Come to Me, all you who labor and are heavy laden, and I will give you rest. Take My yoke upon you and learn from Me, for I am gentle and lowly in heart, and you will find rest for your souls. For My yoke is easy and My burden is light. (Matthew 11:28–30)

6
PRESCRIPTIONS FOR LIFE
Spiritual Medicine to Cure
Whatever Ails You

I grew up in a family of five children with two hardworking parents. My mother worked outside the home after the children were old enough to be in school all day. I had working grandparents, too, so if any of the children became sick and had to stay home, it was very difficult to find a sitter who could take care of us. Therefore, my mother did everything she could to try to prevent us from becoming ill. The highest absenteeism in elementary and secondary schools occurs during the late fall, which is typically cold and flu season. That is why, early in November, Mom would line us up in the kitchen to give us what she called "preventive medicine." Every year, when I heard her calling us to come and take this medicine, my mouth would become dry and my knees would tremble, because I knew what was coming.

"*PREVENTIVE MEDICINE*"

Mom would open a large wooden cabinet door that housed mismatched plates and saucers and draw out a bottle of cod-liver oil that looked to me as large as a half gallon jug of milk. Then she would open the utensil drawer and pull out a spoon that seemed the size of a garden shovel. I always wished my mother would use a teaspoon or eyedropper for that cod-liver oil, but I guess she thought a large dosage was called for.

My brothers and sisters and I would stand in line according to age, looking like stair steps, as we waited for the dreaded medicine. I was the next to the oldest child in my family, so I was second in line. My eyes would fill with tears as I anticipated that awful taste. One would think I would have become used to this ordeal after many years of "preventive medicine." Instead, I hated cod-liver oil so much that I gladly would have traded a bout with the flu to keep from having that fishy taste in my mouth all day.

But each year, my turn came. My older brother Ron would be in the bathroom coughing and gagging after receiving his dosage. I would stand there for a second, praying that my mother would change her mind. "Open wide," she would say, as if I needed instructions. I would step forward, look up, lean my head back, close my eyes, and receive that awful spoonful of cod-liver oil. At first I would hold the medicine in my mouth for a moment, hoping I wouldn't have

GOD'S STRONG MEDICINE IS A SIGN OF HIS LOVE AND CARE.

to swallow it after all. Then it would slide down my throat, and my whole body would shudder.

Mom would not let us drink water after the dosage. She said it would weaken the effect. She would give us a cracker to push the medicine down, but all the cracker did was stick to the oil that coated our mouths. "That's strong medicine," she would say, "and it's good *for* you even if it's not good *to* you." Now I know that she was right and that, when she gave us her "preventive medicine," it was a demonstration of her love and care for us.

Sometimes God's prescriptions for successful living remind me of those dosages of cod-liver oil. His *strong medicine* is not always to our liking. It can involve challenges, humility, self-denial, sacrifice, and perseverance. However, it is *always* good for us. Sooner or later, when we come through our trials victoriously, we will realize that God is demonstrating His love for us and acting in our best interests when He prescribes His time-tested medicine for our difficulties.

153

Strong Medicine

Our Great Physician

So far, we have learned how to identify and face our adversities, and we have discovered that we have an excellent spiritual prognosis in Christ as we depend on Him. Now we are ready to look at some prescriptions of *strong medicine* from the Word of God that address specific life issues.

Jesus is the Great Physician, and He knows the best medicines for all our trials and troubles. We do not need to be afraid to go to Him with any of our difficulties, because He came to help those who are spiritually sick and suffering.

> And their scribes and the Pharisees complained against His disciples, saying, "Why do You eat and drink with tax collectors and sinners?" Jesus answered and said to them, "Those who are well have no need of a physician, but those who are sick. I have not come to call the righteous, but sinners, to repentance." (Luke 5:30)

Specific Prescriptions

Aspirin and other over-the-counter pain relievers are usually able to address the symptoms of a wide range of minor ailments. However, if you have more than just a cold, headache, or mild muscle pain, you need medicine that you can obtain only through a prescription from a physician—medicine that targets your specific ailment and symptoms.

Likewise, while there are certain general truths in the Word of God that apply to a wide range of problems, Scripture also addresses particular areas in which your life can come under attack. Since Jesus is the expert Diagnostician, His prescriptions, which you receive through prayer, the Word of God, and godly counsel, are custom-designed for your specific needs. Receiving and applying these prescriptions are essential steps to your living a successful Christian life. The medicines Jesus gives you are not just "over-the-counter brands" that are designed to address a variety of complaints; rather, they target your particular trials and struggles. That is why they are referred to in this chapter as *prescriptions* and not just "remedies." They are prescribed by the Physician of Physicians for the personal needs of His

154

"patients." Christ pays close attention to those under His care. He always ministers to us with dignity as He addresses our needs.

ADDRESSING ROOT CAUSES

When we fail to address problem areas in our lives, it is often because we do not want to look at their root causes and the spirit that is behind them—such as the spirit of pride, the spirit of bitterness, or the spirit of self-pity. I am not saying that there are demons or evil spirits called "pride," "bitterness," and "self-pity" that take over a person against his or her will; rather, these instigators of our problems are fleshly responses and emotions that we can cultivate in our lives—often unknowingly. They are demonic in the sense that they are not the fruit of the Spirit of God but the fruit of our fallen nature, and when we nurture them, we allow them to become rooted in our spirits. When we give them a place in our lives, we permit our fleshly nature free reign in those areas. This allowance on our part gives the devil a "foothold" to do additional spiritual damage. (See Ephesians 4:27 NIV.) In order to prevent this process from occurring, we need to root out the underlying causes of our difficulties.

WEED PULLING

I find it fascinating that, whenever my husband and I mow the weeds on our lawn, no matter how well we do the job, the weeds always come back. They usually come back strong and hardy, and they try to overwhelm our otherwise beautiful lawn. To get rid of those weeds, we have to dig out their roots. Doing so takes more work than just surface mowing, and so we have to make the time to properly attend to our lawn. The weeds will not go away on their own; neither will they disappear if we remove just the surface evidence of their presence.

The same principle is true in our spiritual lives. Various traumas, such as anger, hurt, distrust, and abandonment, especially when planted within us early in our lives, are like weeds with stubborn roots. These spiritual weeds are fertilized by additional crises in our families of origin, and they fully mature in our adult lives if they are not attended to properly. They choke the life out of our potential and our relationships, marring the life that God intends for us. If we ignore them, or if we make only a surface attempt to eradicate them, they will eventually overtake every good thing we have, and our lives will become like barren fields. When I think about some of the incomplete treatments we as Christians try to apply to our problems, I become concerned that so much of what we are doing is like a futile effort at mowing weeds. God's *strong medicine,* in contrast, pulls up the spiritual roots of our problems so that they can be eradicated from our lives.

INCOMPLETE TREATMENTS ARE LIKE FUTILE ATTEMPTS AT WEED PULLING.

Pulling up these spiritual roots takes a commitment of prayer, time, and follow-through, so that our application of God's truths to our lives can be true medicine and not just an "exercise" that we do. This point is key to God's *strong medicine* being effective for the specific needs in your life. Just because a friend of yours goes to the doctor and is given a prescription for a headache doesn't mean that you should skip going to the doctor yourself and just take your friend's medicine. You need to seek what God is saying to you about your particular difficulty. When the Word is misapplied, it is like taking someone else's prescription, and that practice can yield very harmful results.

SPIRITUAL TREATMENT PLANS

Doctors develop medical treatment plans to improve and maintain the health of their patients. Similarly, God has provided us with "spiritual treatment plans" in the form of truths, principles, and examples in His Word. These treatment plans enable us to diagnose the nature of our trials and to receive God's healing and preventative medicine. This chapter outlines twelve such spiritual treatment plans. I encourage you to apply them to your current situation, study them to prepare for future needs that will likely arise, and use them to strengthen fellow believers who are undergoing trials.

These spiritual treatment plans will help you understand the root causes of your difficulties so that you can receive and apply God's *strong medicine* to them. Consulting a licensed professional or spiritual counselor is helpful—and may be necessary—as you deal with specific medical, emotional, and spiritual issues. However, professional help alone is not sufficient, because it does not always address the *spiritual* root causes of our trials or provide for personal reflection on our problems based on the truth of God's Word. It takes God's *strong medicine* to uncover these root causes and to help us see our problems from His perspective.

Each spiritual treatment plan will provide you with biblical truths and principles pertaining to a specific area of difficulty. The symptoms that often indicate the difficulty are listed. Thought-provoking questions are then included to help you personalize the biblical principles provided, because asking yourself key questions about how you are feeling and how you are reacting to your adversity can help you arrive at a spiritual treatment plan more quickly. These questions are followed by a spiritual diagnosis and a prescription of God's *strong medicine* in the form of Scripture, prayer, and action steps. A prognosis and case study from the Word of God are also provided so that you can make the strongest application of God's medicine to your life.

Working through the spiritual treatment plans, talking with a pastor or counselor who is strong in the Lord, and consulting a licensed professional as needed will help you to gain a well-balanced perspective and receive good counsel about your situation.

I invite you to pray this prayer as you begin to apply God's *strong medicine* in your life.

> *Lord, thank You that You have provided me with strong and effective prescriptions in Your Word for all of my needs. I ask You to help me make the commitment and take the time to discover the root causes of my problems and to apply the appropriate spiritual medicine to them. Guide me as I study the truths and principles from Your Word and learn from the examples of others who have gone through difficulties. Please give me a willing spirit to accept what You want to tell me, and to apply it to my life, so that I may receive full healing. In Jesus' name, Amen.*

Rx *Strong Medicine for*

DISAPPOINTMENT *and* DEPRESSION

Presenting Symptoms:
Sadness; discouragement; hopelessness; feelings of defeat; repressed anger; suicidal thoughts.

Patient Information (Answer the following questions):
➢ What event/person triggered your feelings of disappointment and depression, and why?
➢ Are you feeling hopeless about the general course of your life?
➢ Are you physically, emotionally, or mentally exhausted?
➢ Have you had other similar disappointments in the past, and what were they?
➢ Have you felt anxiety or impatience from having to wait on God, and how did you respond to these feelings?
➢ Have you felt an overwhelming sadness in the last several weeks?

Diagnosis:
Loss of hope in God's faithfulness and power to carry out His promises, combined with self-pity.

Prescription:

God's Word:
➢ *"With God all things are possible"* (Matthew 19:26).
➢ *"Being fully convinced that what He had promised He was also able to perform"* (Romans 4:21).

Prayer: Lord God, forgive me for doubting Your love, faithfulness, and power. Fill me with your joy as I trust in You. Thank you for fulfilling all Your promises and Your will in my life. Amen.

Action Steps:
Practice bringing your thought life in line with God's Word. Whenever you are tempted to doubt the promises, faithfulness, or power of God, repeat the above prayer and Scripture verses. If you are spiritually or physically exhausted, take some time for rest and renewal and remind yourself of the experience of Sarah in the case history that follows from the Word of God.

Prognosis:
Excellent. Symptoms of disappointment and depression due to life's circumstances are temporary if you address their underlying causes—unbelief and lack of trust in God—by leaning fully on God's promises and faithfulness.

CASE HISTORY FROM THE WORD OF GOD:
Sarah, Wife of the Patriarch Abraham
(See Genesis 15:1–18:15; 21:1–7.)

Sarah, an elderly woman who was barren, suffered from deep disappointment. She and her husband had received a promise from God that they would have a son who would be conceived and born naturally. After waiting many years for the fulfillment of this promise without receiving it, Sarah developed feelings of hopelessness over her failed expectations. During this time, she also measured her self-worth on her ability (or lack of ability) to bear a child.

GOD'S TIMING IS ALL-IMPORTANT.

Sarah's attempts at relieving her pain included giving her maidservant Hagar to her husband so that she and Abraham could have a child using a surrogate mother. This union resulted in the birth of a son, whom they named Ishmael. When Hagar became haughty and Sarah became jealous over the surrogate's ability to bear a child, the relationship between the two women disintegrated and was never fully restored. The incident with Hagar only heightened Sarah's distress, rather than relieving it.

The years went by, and then Abraham and Sarah received a confirmation from God about the promise. Sarah's response was to laugh in disbelief and continued despair. Yet a year later, when Sarah was ninety and Abraham was a hundred years old, Sarah gave birth naturally to a son, whom they named Isaac, meaning "laughter." Her bitter disappointment turned to joyful laughter at the miraculous fulfillment of the promise.

Sarah's disappointment was caused by her trusting in circumstances rather than on God's ability and faithfulness to do what He had promised. She took matters into her own hands, causing herself additional grief, but God was true to His word and fulfilled His promise to her. Her life shows us that God's timing is all-important in the fulfillment of His promises to us, and that we are to continue to trust Him even when our circumstances look bad.

Rx STRONG MEDICINE for LOW SELF-ESTEEM

Presenting Symptoms:
Self-doubt; self-contempt; questioning one's intrinsic worth; dissatisfaction with oneself.

Patient Information (Answer the following questions):
➤ On what do you determine your value and self-worth?
➤ Do you compare yourself to others and their abilities and accomplishments?
➤ What qualities and abilities do you value?
➤ What qualities and abilities does the Bible value?
➤ What does it mean to be a child of God?
➤ What are your God-given strengths?
➤ What areas of your life would you like to change, with God's help?

Diagnosis:
Lack of understanding of what it means to be a child of God and to be called according to His purposes.

Prescription:

God's Word:
➤ *"I will praise You, for I am fearfully and wonderfully made; marvelous are Your works"* (Psalm 139:14).
➤ *"We are His workmanship, created in Christ Jesus for good works"* (Ephesians 2:10).

Prayer: Lord, forgive me for determining my value and self-worth by comparing myself with others rather than by my position as Your child and the gifts and abilities You have given me. Help me to see myself as You do. Show me the spiritual gifts and talents You have placed within me and enable me to use them for Your glory. Amen.

Action Steps:
Practice bringing your thought life in line with God's Word. Whenever you are tempted to doubt your own worth, repeat the above prayer and Scripture verses. If you are spiritually or physically exhausted, take some time for rest and renewal, then remind yourself of the experience of the Israelite spies in the case history that follows from the Word of God.

160

Prognosis:

Extraordinary. Symptoms of a lack of self-esteem can be cured if you address their underlying cause—comparing yourself with others rather than seeing yourself as God sees you—by acknowledging you are a child of God and that He will fulfill His purposes in you.

CASE HISTORY FROM THE WORD OF GOD:
The Israelite Spies
(See Numbers 13:1–14:9.)

When God delivered the Israelites from Egypt and promised them the land of Canaan as their inheritance, He instructed Moses to send spies to survey the land. One spy from each of the twelve tribes of Israel was chosen, all of them leaders in their respective tribes. When the spies returned, they told the people the land was prosperous and the soil was exceptional; they brought back a huge cluster of grapes and other fruit as evidence.

SEE YOURSELF THROUGH GOD'S EYES.

However, most of the spies said it was no use trying to take the land because the Canaanites were strong and their cities were large and fortified. They said, *"We were like grasshoppers in our own sight, and so we were in their sight"* (vv. 32–33). Only Caleb and Joshua disagreed, saying they should immediately take possession of the land because God had promised to give it to them.

The Israelites believed the bad report of the other ten spies. They wanted to stone Caleb and Joshua, replace Moses with a new leader, and return to Egypt—but God intervened. God was exceedingly angry with them for their unbelief. He said they would die in the desert and only their descendants would enter Canaan.

The first-generation Israelites' failure to enter the Promised Land was caused by a poor self-concept. Their ability to take the land was never the real question. *They* could not take the land, but God could, and He had promised to give it to them. The Israelites (1) based their worth on their own abilities rather than on God's ability; (2) looked at the outward appearances of the Canaanites' strength and resources, rather than on God's power and faithfulness; (3) failed to identify themselves as God's people; (4) discounted the qualities of faith and trust that Caleb and Joshua had, and which they could have had, as well.

The ten faithless spies had been chosen because they had been dependable, capable men up to that point, leaders of their communities. Yet they did not see themselves as God saw them and therefore made a fatal decision that affected the destiny of a nation. Only Joshua and Caleb, who proved faithful, saw themselves from God's point of view and entered the Promised Land.

Rx STRONG MEDICINE *for* LONELINESS

Presenting Symptoms:
Feelings of isolation and abandonment; fear of having to face the difficulties of life alone.

Patient Information (Answer the following questions):
➢ What is causing you to feel alone?
➢ Are you carrying an overwhelming load of responsibility instead of asking others to help you?
➢ Have you recently had to stand alone in a situation involving speaking the truth or doing the right thing?
➢ Do you attend a church regularly?
➢ Do you have someone to talk to about your life and problems?
➢ Have you been reading God's Word and praying to Him?
➢ Does your relationship with the Lord need to be restored or deepened?

Diagnosis:
Forgetfulness of God's promise never to leave His people, and a lack of fellowship with God and/or other believers.

Prescription:

God's Word:
➢ *"I am with you always, even to the end of the age"* (Matthew 28:20).
➢ *"The grace of the Lord Jesus Christ, and the love of God, and the communion of the Holy Spirit be with you"* (2 Corinthians 13:14).

Prayer:
Lord, I'm feeling very lonely. Please help me to hold onto Your promise always to be with me. Enable me to find fellowship with strong Christians who love You and will pray for me and give me spiritual support. I ask You to comfort me with the peace and presence of the Holy Spirit. In Jesus' name, Amen.

Action Steps:
Practice bringing your thought life in line with God's Word. Whenever you begin to feel lonely, repeat the above prayer and Scripture verses. If you are spiritually or physically exhausted, take some time for rest and renewal, then remind yourself of the experience of Elijah in the case history that follows from the Word of God.

Prognosis:
Outstanding. Symptoms of loneliness can be cured if you first recognize their underlying causes—losing sight of the fact that God is always with you and the importance of regular fellowship with other believers. Then they can be addressed by trusting in God's presence in your life and joining with other believers for worship, prayer, and mutual encouragement.

CASE HISTORY FROM THE WORD OF GOD:
Elijah the Prophet
(See 1 Kings 18:21–19:18.)

Elijah had been sent by God to challenge the prophets of the false god Baal. The prophet had been an integral part of God's striking victory over Baal by calling down fire from heaven, which utterly consumed the sacrifices to the false deity, and killing all the false prophets. Elijah had obeyed God and fulfilled His will with great success. Yet when Jezebel, the wicked wife of evil king Ahab, immediately threatened to kill him, he *"ran for his life"* (v. 3), traveled deep into the desert, and prayed to God that he might die.

God knew Elijah was exhausted from his exploits with the Baal prophets and his long journey, so He allowed him to rest and gave him something to eat. However, Elijah ran even farther away from God. The word of the Lord then came to him, asking, *"What are you doing here, Elijah?"* (v. 9). Elijah explained that he had been zealous for the Lord, but that now he was the only one left alive who was a true follower of God and that Ahab and Jezebel wanted to kill him. God assured Elijah that he was not alone and that there were seven thousand Israelites who were still faithful to Him.

Elijah was lonely for several reasons. First, he was exhausted; therefore, the new challenge from Jezebel seemed overwhelming; he thought he had to face her threats alone. Elijah also took too much responsibility upon himself instead of relying on God. He had an exaggerated sense of his own importance in accomplishing God's purposes. If he had been more in tune with how God was working, he would have realized he was not the sole follower of God left in Israel. Yet God renewed Elijah's spiritual life by teaching him that He was still very much in control and that He always reserves a remnant of people who will faithfully serve Him. No matter what we are going through, God is always with us, and He will provide us with spiritual strength and refreshment. He has many ways to accomplish His purposes. While we are important to those purposes, we shouldn't think that everything will fall apart if we are not personally involved in all of them.

GOD IS WITH YOU.

$R\!x$ STRONG MEDICINE *for* FEAR

Presenting Symptoms:

Apprehension of the past, present, or future; feelings of anxiety, worry, or dread; lack of peace.

Patient Information (Answer the following questions):

➤ What do you fear, and why?
➤ When you are asked to do something new or challenging, how do you react?
➤ Do certain past or future events make you afraid?
➤ Would you describe yourself as a worrier?
➤ Have you been told you expect too much from yourself?
➤ Have you entrusted your life and the lives of those you love to God's care?

Diagnosis:

Lack of understanding that God has promised to carry your burdens and will enable you to do all He has called you to do.

Prescription:

God's Word:
➤ *"Be anxious for nothing, but in everything by prayer and supplication, with thanksgiving, let your requests be made known to God; and the peace of God...will guard your hearts and minds through Christ Jesus"* (Philippians 4:6–7).
➤ *"Casting all your care upon Him, for He cares for you"* (1 Peter 5:7).

Prayer:

God, please forgive me for looking at my own abilities and circumstances instead of Your strength, which is made perfect in my weaknesses. Help me to cast all my worries upon You and to commit my life and the lives of those I love to your faithful care. I acknowledge you as my Strength and my Redeemer. Amen.

Action Steps:

Practice bringing your thought life in line with God's Word. Whenever you begin to feel afraid, repeat the above prayer and Scripture verses. If you are spiritually or physically exhausted, take some time for rest and renewal, then remind yourself of the story of the parting of the Red Sea in the case history that follows from the Word of God.

Prognosis:

Marvelous. Symptoms of fear can be cured if you address their underlying causes—carrying your own burdens and not allowing God to help you fulfill your calling in life—by trusting Him to take care of your needs and to accomplish His purposes in you.

CASE HISTORY FROM THE WORD OF GOD:
The Parting of the Red Sea

(See Exodus 14:1–22.)

The Hebrew people were cruelly oppressed as slaves in Egypt for four hundred years. Through a series of miraculous events, a Hebrew baby named Moses became a prince in the court of Pharaoh, Egypt's king. However, when Moses began to identify with his own people and tried to help them, he was forced to flee, becoming an outcast in a desert land. Years later, God called Moses to return to Egypt to lead His people out of slavery. So

> GOD CAN OPEN UP A WAY.

Moses went back to Egypt and confronted Pharaoh, telling him to free the Hebrew slaves or suffer God's wrath in the form of plagues. Pharaoh made the Egyptians suffer through ten plagues while he kept making and breaking his promises to release the Israelites. Finally, after the death of the firstborn of every Egyptian family, Pharaoh agreed to let the Hebrews leave. Yet as soon as they had left, he changed his mind and pursued them.

The children of Israel, who were encamped near the Red Sea, saw Pharaoh and his army approaching them in the distance. Six hundred Egyptian war chariots were bearing down on the Israelites, who were trapped between the mountains and the Red Sea. The people cried out to the Lord in terror, but Moses told them, "Don't be afraid. Just stand where you are and watch, and you will see the wonderful way the Lord will rescue you today." The Lord then told Moses, "Lift your rod and hold it over the water. The sea will open up a path before you, and the people of Israel will walk through on dry ground." When there had been no way of escape, the Lord miraculously delivered the Israelites once again.

Sometimes you, too, will find yourself in a situation in which you feel trapped. Don't panic: God can open up a way of escape. The Israelites' response to their crisis was fear and despair. From a natural standpoint, being pursued by the Egyptian army would be terrifying, but the Israelites had just seen God's powerful hand free them from slavery. If they had trusted in His character and past performance, they would have known He would not allow the Egyptians to destroy them. Similarly, by focusing on God's faithfulness to you in the past, you can avoid responding to your crises with fear. You can adopt Moses' attitude—"Watch and see what God will do"—and experience His strong deliverance.

165

Rx STRONG MEDICINE for

PAINFUL MEMORIES and GUILT

Presenting Symptoms:
Guilt, shame, regret, or sorrow from *experiencing* or *causing* certain past events.

Patient Information (Answer the following questions):
- ➤ What painful memories are you experiencing?
- ➤ Are you able to forgive yourself for past mistakes?
- ➤ Are you burdened with guilt and shame for past mistakes?
- ➤ Do guilt and shame keep you from moving forward in your life?
- ➤ Have you forgiven those who have wronged you?
- ➤ Have you asked God to forgive you for your past mistakes?
- ➤ Have you asked others to forgive you for hurting them?

Diagnosis:
Lack of living in God's forgiveness and of believing that God can use even past painful experiences for your good.

Prescription:

God's Word:
- ➤ *"Therefore, if anyone is in Christ, he is a new creation; old things have passed away; behold, all things have become new"* (2 Corinthians 5:17).
- ➤ *"All things work together for good to those who love God, to those who are the called according to His purpose"* (Romans 8:28).

Prayer:
Lord, I offer all my painful memories to you. Please enable me to forgive myself and others for causing my pain. I ask you to strengthen my faith to believe that you can use even the hurtful experiences of my life for my good. Let me find refuge in your love, comfort, and peace. In Jesus' name, I pray. Amen.

Action Steps:
Practice bringing your thought life in line with God's Word. Whenever painful memories come to mind, repeat the above prayer and Scripture verses. If you are spiritually or physically exhausted, take some time for rest and renewal, then remind yourself of the life of the apostle Paul in the case history that follows from the Word of God.

Prognosis:
Superb. Painful memories can be healed if you address their underlying cause—holding onto the past—by living in God's forgiveness and believing He can use all things for your good.

CASE HISTORY FROM THE WORD OF GOD:
The Apostle Paul
(See Acts 7:58–8:3; 9:1–22; Philippians 3:4–7.)

Before Paul gave his life to Christ, he severely persecuted the Christians—harassing, jailing, and murdering them for their faith. Paul was a Pharisee, a religious leader of the Jews. His actions were based on his zeal to protect God's name from those he considered heretical. He thought he was doing the right thing in hunting down and killing Christians.

When Christ revealed His glory to Paul on the road to Damascus, Paul realized he had made a grave mistake. Jesus had come to fulfill—not destroy—the covenant that God had made with Abraham. Jesus was his Messiah. Paul went on to be a great apostle, missionary to the Gentiles, and author of the majority of the New Testament. Yet think about how he must have felt when he first realized what he had done. Through his actions, he had persecuted

SEEK GOD'S FORGIVENESS, RECONCILIATION, AND PURPOSE.

Christ and put God's people to death. Their blood was on his hands. Some believers had probably even renounced their faith as a result of his persecution. How could he live with himself?

Paul was able to release the painful memories of his past for several reasons. First, God granted him *forgiveness*. Only Christ's death on the cross could have atoned for Paul's terrible sins—however ignorantly they were committed—and restore him to God. Second, God brought about *reconciliation* between Paul and those he had formerly persecuted. Stephen had asked God to forgive those who were involved in killing him—including Paul. This believer's forgiveness paved the way for Paul's reconciliation with God. Ananias, who once had been terrified of Paul, referred to him as "brother" when God instructed him to pray for Paul's healing. Ananias's obedience to God paved the way for Paul's acceptance in the church. Third, God gave Paul *new purpose* in life, assigning him the special task of apostle. Rather than dwelling in despair over his past, Paul embraced the new role God had given him and moved forward in His will and purpose for his life. Likewise, forgiveness, reconciliation, and purpose in Christ will enable you to put your painful memories behind you.

Rx STRONG MEDICINE for
ANGER, BITTERNESS, and UNFORGIVENESS

Presenting Symptoms:
Resentment; rage; hostility; hatefulness; holding grudges; speaking evil of others; unwillingness to forgive.

Patient Information (Answer the following questions):
➤ What person(s) or circumstance are you angry or bitter about?
➤ How has your anger or bitterness affected your life?
➤ Are you able to pray for the person/situation you are angry about?
➤ Do you feel physical discomfort when you see/think about the person(s) who wronged you?
➤ Do you find it difficult to forgive others?
➤ Do you hang onto grudges long after you have forgotten why you were angry in the first place?

Diagnosis:
Unwillingness to forgive those who have wronged you or who have wronged those you care about.

Prescription:

God's Word:
➤ *"If you forgive men their trespasses, your heavenly Father will also forgive you"* (Matthew 6:14).
➤ *"Let all bitterness, wrath, anger, clamor, and evil speaking be put away from you, with all malice"* (Ephesians 4:31).

Prayer:
Lord, I have to admit how angry I am about this circumstance. I don't have any desire to forgive those involved, but I ask You to change my heart. Please let the Spirit of Christ reign in my life so that I can live in Your love and forgiveness and so that You can use this situation for my good and Your glory. Amen.

Action Steps:
Practice bringing your thought life in line with God's Word. Whenever you feel angry, bitter, or resentful, repeat the above prayer and Scripture verses. If you are spiritually or physically exhausted, take some time for rest and renewal, then remind yourself of the experience of Jonah in the case history that follows from the Word of God.

Prognosis:
Superior. Anger or resentment can be healed if you address its underlying cause—unforgiveness—by extending forgiveness and always looking at your life and relationships from God's perspective.

CASE HISTORY FROM THE WORD OF GOD:
The Prophet Jonah
(See the book of Jonah.)

Jonah was *angry.* What kind of assignment was God giving him? Was he to preach repentance to the vile, pagan Ninevites? He wanted them to be wiped out, not forgiven. Jonah knew that God would spare the Ninevites if they repented, and so, instead of obeying God, he ran away and boarded a ship headed for Tarshish.

However, God caused a great storm to arise that threatened to sink the ship. The sailors were terrified, and Jonah knew he was the cause of their distress. He told them to throw him overboard so that the storm would stop. When they did, God sent a great fish to swallow Jonah, who lived for three days in the belly of that fish. When he cried out to God, the fish vomited him onto dry land. Then God spoke to Jonah a second time

UNFORGIVENESS IS REALLY SELFISHNESS.

about going to Nineveh. This time, Jonah obeyed, went to Nineveh, and warned the Ninevites about God's impending judgment on them for their wickedness. The entire city repented, and God in His mercy spared the city from destruction.

Now Jonah was *really* angry. This result was the very reason He hadn't wanted to go to Nineveh in the first place. He was so infuriated that he said he wanted to die. Jonah went outside the gates of the city to keep watch and see if God would change His mind about sparing the Ninevites. The sun was blistering hot, but God caused a plant to grow tall and give Jonah shade, for which Jonah was very grateful. The next day, God caused it to wither, and Jonah became so hot that he again said he wanted to die. God asked him if he had a right to feel that way. Jonah replied, *"It is right for me to be angry, even to death!"* (Jonah 4:9). Then God told Jonah that while he was feeling sorry for the loss of the plant, he should have been grieving over the lost state of the Ninevites, who would die in their sins if He did not show them mercy.

Jonah's experience reveals that when we hold onto anger about others or about our circumstances, we are looking at things from a selfish perspective. God wants to restore all people to Himself. Our anger may be preventing us from praying for others and from having the fullness of life in God that He desires for us.

Rx *Strong Medicine for Illness*

Presenting Symptoms:
Physical weakness or frailty; sickness; disease; infirmity.

Patient Information (Answer the following questions):
- What is the nature of your illness?
- Have you committed your sickness to the Great Physician and sought His guidance about your situation?
- Have you sought medical help, and have you followed through with the doctor's instructions for healing?
- Have you been anointed and prayed for by the leaders of your church, according to James 5:14–15?
- Do you blame God for your illness?
- Have you applied the Word of God to your life in faith?
- What has God shown you through your illness?

Diagnosis:
The body's failure to maintain health due to living in a fallen world with ever present diseases, attacks from the enemy, and the consequences of poor lifestyle choices.

Prescription:

God's Word:
- *"I am the LORD who heals you"* (Exodus 15:26).
- *"He was wounded for our transgressions, He was bruised for our iniquities; the chastisement for our peace was upon Him, and by His stripes we are healed"* (Isaiah 53:5)

Prayer:
Lord, You know all about my illness. I ask You to give me wisdom about my situation and healing for my spirit, mind, and body. Show me all that You want to teach me during the time of my illness, and enable me to exercise strong faith in You in the midst of it. Thank you for Your love and care for me during my affliction. In the name of Jesus, I pray. Amen.

Action Steps:
Practice bringing your thought life in line with God's Word. Whenever you are ill, repeat the above prayer and Scripture verses. If you are spiritually or physically exhausted, take time for rest and renewal, then remind yourself of the experience of the woman with the issue of blood in the case history that follows from the Word of God.

Prognosis:
Superlative. The symptoms of physical illness can be addressed, first, by recognizing their root cause—sin in the earth; second, by receiving medical help; third, and most importantly, by acknowledging God as your Healer, committing your situation to Him, receiving His guidance, and relying on His Word in faith.

CASE HISTORY FROM THE WORD OF GOD:
The Woman with the Issue of Blood
(See Matthew 9:20–22; Mark 5:25–34; Luke 8:43–48.)

For twelve long years, this woman had suffered from a continual flow of blood. No matter how many doctors she went to, none of them could find the reason for her sickness. Most importantly, they could find no cure for it. She had spent all her savings on these physicians, and she had no money and no hope of ever being healed. Meanwhile, her illness was making her weaker and weaker.

One day, she heard that Jesus was traveling through the countryside, preaching to and healing the people, and she got an idea. "With that kind of power," she reasoned, "all I would have to do is touch His clothes, and I would be made well." She found out where Jesus was and went to see Him. There was a large crowd gathered around Him, but in spite of her weak body, she made her way to Jesus'

JESUS BRINGS HEALING AND PEACE.

side. The woman touched Jesus' garment, and suddenly she knew she had been healed. Her heart filled with overwhelming joy until she heard Jesus say, "Who touched Me?" Though the crowds were pressing all around Him, she knew what He meant—He wanted to know who had received His healing power.

Trembling with fear, she stepped forward and fell at His feet. When she began to speak, all her pent-up emotions poured out. She told Him about her illness, the doctors, and spending all her money. She thought He would be angry at her for her secret action. But Jesus did not reprimand her. He looked at her kindly and said, "Daughter, you do not have to be afraid. Your faith has healed you. Go in peace." All the joy came flooding back into her heart. She managed to whisper, "Thank you," before some men moved forward to talk to Him. Then she ran all the way home, totally healed, laughing and crying at the same time.

The account of this woman's suffering shows us that no matter how advanced our medical technology becomes, no matter how many experts we go to when we are ill, Jesus is the One we are ultimately to go to with our sicknesses. He knows all things, and He has compassion on you in your situation. Entrust your life to Him, pour out your troubles to Him, and let Him respond with a healing touch and peace that only He can give.

Rx *STRONG MEDICINE for GRIEF AND LOSS*

Presenting Symptoms:
Sorrow; anguish; a broken heart; distress over the loss of a loved one; refusing to be consoled.

Patient Information (Answer the following questions):
➤ Have you or someone you know suffered the tragic death of a loved one or the loss of something of great value?
➤ Have you allowed yourself to truly grieve over this loss?
➤ Have you reached out to Jesus in your sorrow as the One *"acquainted with grief"* (Isaiah 53:3)?
➤ Have you read Jesus' reactions to death in Luke 7 and John 11?
➤ Do you feel physical discomfort when you think about your loss?
➤ Are you holding onto someone you lost when it is time to commit the person to God's hands and move forward in your life?

Diagnosis:
The symptoms of grief are a natural response to the tragedy of death and loss. Yet if these symptoms are prolonged, they may indicate a refusal to receive God's comfort and to recognize that He wants to use even this situation for good in your life.

Prescription:

God's Word:
➤ *"The Spirit of the LORD is upon Me, because He has anointed Me to...heal the broken hearted"* (Luke 4:18).
➤ *"God will wipe away every tear from their eyes; there shall be no more death, nor sorrow, nor crying. There shall be no more pain, for the former things have passed away"* (Revelation 21:4).

Prayer:
Lord Jesus, I am overwhelmed with grief and sadness. Please give me your comfort and peace in my anguish. Help me to go through the grieving process and to commit my situation into Your loving hands. Give me renewed strength and courage, and enable me to move forward with my life as I trust in You. Amen.

Action Steps:
Practice bringing your thought life in line with God's Word. Whenever you are grieving over a loss, repeat the above prayer and Scripture verses. If you are spiritually or physically exhausted, take time for rest and renewal, then remind yourself of the experience of the widow of Nain in the case history that follows from the Word of God.

Prognosis:
Extraordinary. The symptoms of grief and loss can be alleviated by recognizing their source—the natural reaction to losing someone or something you love and the tragedy of death—and by acknowledging God's comfort and love for you as He grieves alongside you.

CASE HISTORY FROM THE WORD OF GOD:
The Widow of Nain
(See Luke 7:11–15.)

The widow's son was the only family she had left. When he became ill and died, her heart was crushed by the weight of the loss. She did not know how she could possibly go on, yet she still had to go through the ordeal of burying him.

The funeral procession moved slowly through the city, passing all the places her son had played when he was a boy. She used to like this city of Nain, which meant "pleasant." Now it was anything but pleasant to her. So many people from the city came to grieve with her, and she was grateful for their concern, but she just wanted to be alone with her loss. She thought her heart would truly break as she stumbled along, blinded by tears, holding tightly to the funeral bier as her last contact with her beloved son.

She vaguely noticed another large crowd approaching them from outside the city. When the funeral procession passed through the city gates headed for the grave, a Man from that crowd came forward to speak to her. She looked up at Him through her tears and saw deep compassion and sadness in His eyes. Gently, He said, "Do not weep." Before she could reply, He walked over to the funeral bier and touched it. The men who were carrying it stopped walking, and both crowds of people stood still. Then this Man said to her son, "Young man, get up." Her son opened his eyes, sat up, and began to speak! She was too stunned to respond. This was, after all, a terribly bittersweet dream from which she would soon awaken. But then the Man said, "Here is your son," and she felt her son's arms embracing her and knew that it was really true. He was alive!

JESUS GRIEVES WITH US.

The story of the widow of Nain reveals that although death and loss come to everyone because of our fallen world, Jesus never takes them lightly. All of our anguish is felt by our loving Savior, and He has compassion on us. When you experience grief, you can reach out to Him, knowing that He understands and desires to bring you deep comfort. He dries our tears with the promise that there will be no more death, sorrow, pain, or crying because He has conquered them forever through His own death and resurrection (Revelation 21:4).

173

Rx *STRONG MEDICINE for a BROKEN RELATIONSHIP*

Presenting Symptoms:
Emotional separation from or breakdown in communication with a relative, friend, or colleague; marital separation or divorce; severing of shared lives, thoughts, and love with a significant person in your life.

Patient Information (Answer the following questions):
➤ Have you done your part by taking steps to restore the broken relationships in your life?
➤ Have you asked for forgiveness from those you have wronged?
➤ When you have been mistreated by others, how have you reacted?
➤ Have you forgiven others as Christ has forgiven you?
➤ Are you praying for your enemies and others with whom you are in conflict?
➤ Have you asked God to bring reconciliation and to use broken relationships for good in the lives of those involved?

Diagnosis:
Lack of applying God's principles of kindness, forbearance, and forgiveness toward others.

Prescription:

God's Word:
➤ *"If it is possible, as much as depends on you, live peaceably with all men"* (Romans 12:18).
➤ *"And be kind to one another, tenderhearted, forgiving one another, just as God in Christ forgave you"* (Ephesians 4:32).

Prayer:
Lord Jesus, these relationships in my life are broken. I ask You to help me to do my part in restoring them. Please give me a forgiving heart and enable me to ask for forgiveness from those I have wronged. Thank You for bringing reconciliation to these relationships, just as You have reconciled me to God. Amen.

Action Steps:
Practice bringing your thought life in line with God's Word. Whenever you face a broken relationship, repeat the above prayer and Scripture verses. If you are spiritually or physically exhausted, take time for rest and renewal, then remind yourself of the experience of Joseph in the case history that follows from the Word of God.

Prognosis:
Excellent. The symptoms of a broken relationship can be healed or at least dealt with by one party by addressing their source—lack of forbearance and unforgiveness—and by acknowledging God's power to bring restoration and blessing in the lives of those involved.

CASE HISTORY FROM THE WORD OF GOD:
Joseph Sold into Slavery by His Brothers
(See Genesis 37; 39:1–47:11; 49:33–50:22.)

Joseph was despised by his brothers because their father Jacob favored him. God had a special plan for Joseph's life, but Joseph was still young and immature. When he had two prophetic dreams that depicted his father, mother, and brothers bowing down to him, he unwisely told his family the content of these dreams. This revelation prompted a reprimand from his father but produced deep animosity in his brothers.

One day, when Joseph went to see how his brothers were doing as they tended the family flock, his brothers decided to get rid of him. Originally planning to kill him, they ended up selling him into slavery. When the brothers went home, they told Jacob a wild animal had killed Joseph. Meanwhile, Joseph ended up as a slave in Egypt, but God blessed him with remarkable success. Although he experienced hardship and misfortune, he ended up becoming Pharaoh's second in command. He was made overseer of the entire nation, and he received wisdom from God that saved Egypt and its surrounding nations from starvation during a severe famine.

Jacob and his family were suffering because of the same famine, so Joseph's brothers went to Egypt to purchase food. Joseph recognized them, but they did not recognize him. Joseph had experienced God's favor, and he recognized that God had allowed him to be sold into slavery for His greater purposes. He did not resent his brothers but loved them and desired to be reconciled. Yet he tested his brothers to see if they had **GOD MEANT IT FOR GOOD.** changed. When he learned they had matured, he revealed his identity. A poignant reconciliation followed, in which Joseph assured them of his forgiveness. They, along with Jacob, moved to Egypt, and Joseph provided for them.

When Jacob died, the brothers were afraid that Joseph would finally take revenge on them. Joseph wept because they were still living in fear. He told them, *"Do not be afraid....You meant evil against me; but God meant it for good, in order to...save many people"* (Genesis 50:19–20). Joseph knew that reconciliation is based on God's mercy and His ability to use bad situations for the good of all involved.

175

Rx STRONG MEDICINE for BETRAYAL AND INFIDELITY

Presenting Symptoms:
Symptoms of Being Betrayed: Deep feelings of rejection, loss, and desertion. *Symptoms of Infidelity:* Faithlessness; disloyalty; treachery; desertion; defaulting on a moral or spiritual obligation.

Patient Information (Answer the following questions):
➤ Have you been the victim of betrayal or infidelity?
➤ Have you forgiven the one who sinned against you, or have you sought revenge?
➤ Have you betrayed another?
➤ Have you asked forgiveness of the one you betrayed?
➤ Have you asked God's forgiveness for breaking faith with Him?
➤ Do you base your relationships with God and your spouse on covenantal commitment or on your feelings?

Diagnosis:
Deep feelings of rejection and loss are natural reactions to betrayal. However, after these feelings are experienced, if forgiveness is not applied, there may be side effects, such as bitterness and desire for revenge (See Prescriptions for "Anger, Bitterness, and Unforgiveness" and "A Broken Relationship.") The root cause of infidelity is fear and insecurity in relationships, resulting in unfaithfulness and/or a rejection of God's marriage covenant.

Prescription:

God's Word:
➤ *"Let none deal treacherously with the wife* [husband] *of his* [her] *youth"* (Malachi 2:15).
➤ *"You shall love the LORD your God with all your heart, with all your soul, and with all your strength"* (Deuteronomy 6:5).

Prayer for Betrayal:
Lord, heal my hurting heart and feelings of rejection. Grant me your peace as I release those who have offended me. Amen.
Prayer for Infidelity: Lord, forgive me for my disloyalty and infidelity toward my loved one. Deliver me from my fears and insecurities. Grant me a heart of faithfulness, in Jesus' name. Amen.

Action Steps:
Practice bringing your thought life in line with God's Word. If you are involved in a situation of betrayal or infidelity, repeat the above prayer and Scripture verses. If you are spiritually or physically exhausted, take time for rest and renewal, then remind yourself of the experience of David in the case history that follows from the Word of God.

Prognosis:
Outstanding. The symptoms of betrayal and infidelity can be healed or at least dealt with by one party by addressing their source—forsaking the commandment of God to be faithful to Himself and others with whom we are in covenant—and by acknowledging God's power to bring restoration and blessing in the lives of those involved.

CASE HISTORY FROM THE WORD OF GOD:
David and Bathsheba; David and Absalom
(See 2 Samuel 11–12:25; 13–19.)

God called David "a man after His own heart," and David was a great king of Israel. Yet he was on both the giving end and the receiving end of betrayal. First, David betrayed his relationship with God by committing adultery. At a time of idleness in his life, he was attracted to Bathsheba, the wife of Uriah, and had sexual relations with her. When she became pregnant, David had Uriah killed. Then he brought Bathsheba into his house as his wife.

The prophet Nathan came to David and gave him this word from God: *"'Why have you despised the commandment of the LORD, to do evil in His sight? You have killed Uriah the Hittite with the sword; you have taken his wife to be your wife....Now therefore, the sword shall never depart from your house....Behold, I will raise up adversity against you from your own house'"* (2 Samuel 12:9–11). Because David *"despised the commandment of the LORD,"* he would reap what he had sown. His household was plagued with conflicts and tragedies. Yet what grieved him most was the betrayal of his beloved son Absalom, who tried to usurp the crown and succeeded in making David flee for his life. In the end, Absalom was killed, but David greatly mourned his son's death.

The tragic turn of events in David's life shows us that our acts of betrayal and infidelity are not committed in isolation and that there are consequences to our disobedience to God. To David's credit, he immediately repented when God pointed out his sin. His relationship with God was restored, and the Fifty-first Psalm is a record of his prayer for forgiveness and restoration. David also had no desire to take revenge against his son for his betrayal. He commanded that Absalom be kept alive, but Absalom's death was permitted by God because he had tried to take the throne from God's anointed king.

INFIDELITY IS A SIN AGAINST GOD.

Betrayal and infidelity can have terrible consequences, yet God brought good even out of these situations in David's life. Bathsheba became the mother of Solomon, whom God loved and chose to be the next king of Israel. When God delivered David from Absalom, He reaffirmed His everlasting covenant with David, through whose lineage the eternal King, the Messiah, would come.

Rx *Strong Medicine for Addiction*

Presenting Symptoms:
Lack of self-control; compulsive desire or need for something or habitual and obsessive surrender to something, especially something harmful.

Patient Information (Answer the following questions):
➤ Have you developed an addiction by trying to fill a void in your life with food, alcohol, drugs, sex, power, or anything else?
➤ Have you placed your desire for someone or something else above your relationship with God?
➤ Have you asked God to take away your desire for your addiction, and have you recommitted your life to Him?
➤ Are your loved ones being negatively affected by your addiction?
➤ Have you sought professional help for your addiction?
➤ Are you putting yourself in a position where you are tempted to indulge in an addictive behavior?

Diagnosis:
Indulgence in idolatry by putting more value on an object or person for fulfillment and gratification than on your heavenly Father.

Prescription:

God's Word:
➤ *"If anyone desires to come after Me, let him deny himself, and take up his cross, and follow Me"* (Matthew 16:24).
➤ *"Therefore, my beloved, flee from idolatry"* (1 Corinthians 10:14).

Prayer:
Lord, I confess that I have not loved You above all other relationships and things in my life. I have developed addictions that have become idols to me and kept me from a healthy relationship with You. Please forgive me and replace my desire for my addiction with a desire to serve You wholeheartedly. In Jesus' name, Amen.

Action Steps:
Practice bringing your thought life in line with God's Word. Whenever you face a situation of addiction, repeat the above prayer and Scripture verses. If you are spiritually or physically exhausted, take time for rest and renewal, then remind yourself of the rich young ruler in the case history that follows from the Word of God.

Prognosis:
Exceptional. Addiction can be healed if you address its underlying cause—idolatry—and if you commit yourself to God, asking Him to enable you to love Him with all your heart, soul, mind, and strength.

CASE HISTORY FROM THE WORD OF GOD:
The Rich Young Ruler
(See Matthew 19:16–29; Mark 10:17–30; Luke 18:18–30.)

The rich young ruler was waiting for a chance to ask Jesus a question that was burning within him. He had heard Jesus preaching, and he knew that Jesus had great wisdom in the things of God. If he could receive the answer to his question, perhaps his spiritual restlessness could be cured. One day, when he saw Jesus walking along the

AN ADDICTION IS REALLY AN IDOL.

road, he saw his chance. He ran to Jesus, dropped to his knees before Him, and asked, "What should I do to inherit eternal life?" Jesus told him that he should obey the Ten Commandments. He answered that he had kept all the Commandments from the time he was a boy.

Jesus saw the young man's desire to serve God, and He was filled with love for him. He told him how to remove the final barrier that was keeping him from eternal life: "Sell everything you have, give it to the poor, and then take up your cross and follow Me." The young man was stricken; then he stood up and walked away, because he was very rich and did not want to give up his wealth.

The point Jesus was making to the young ruler was not that selling everything you own, in itself, will bring you eternal life, but that it is necessary to commit your whole heart to God to have a genuine relationship with Him. If we love anything more than God, we are committing idolatry. The man had made riches his idol; he worshipped his wealth above God, becoming addicted to it in the process. He was not willing to give it up even to receive eternal life!

People develop addictions when they allow certain things to become idols in their lives. Addiction does not refer only to drugs and alcohol. You can become addicted to anything you idolize and allow to control you, such as money, power, or another person. If there is anything you would not give up if Jesus posed a question to you similar to the one He asked the rich young ruler, then you have a serious problem with your relationship with God that needs to be addressed immediately for the sake of your spiritual health.

Rx STRONG MEDICINE for SPIRITUAL WEARINESS

Presenting Symptoms:
Depletion of spiritual strength and vitality; exhaustion affecting the sharpness and readiness of the mind and spirit to act and react; susceptibility to temptation.

Patient Information (Answer the following questions):
➤ Are you weary from time spent in intense ministry and standing against the enemy?
➤ Have you *made* time in your schedule for spiritual renewal?
➤ Do you know when you need to stop working or ministering and allow God to refresh your spirit?
➤ Are you trying to do too many tasks by yourself in your ministry for the Lord?
➤ Do you have trouble delegating tasks to others?
➤ Do you feel that you are indispensable in your job and that no one else can do it as well?

Diagnosis:
Natural fatigue from prolonged and intense periods of spiritual service or exhaustion from taking on too much responsibility.

Prescription:

God's Word:
➤ *"Great multitudes came together to hear, and to be healed by Him of their infirmities. So He Himself often withdrew into the wilderness and prayed"* (Luke 5:15–16).
➤ *"My yoke is easy and My burden is light"* (Matthew 11:30).

Prayer:
Lord, I confess that I am not very good at slowing down and allowing you to refresh my body, mind, and spirit. Forgive me for trying to minister in Your name while spiritually depleted. Help me to delegate tasks that I do not need to do myself. Please fill me anew with the joy and power of the Holy Spirit so that I can minister in Your strength and not in my weakness. Amen.

Action Steps:
Practice bringing your thought life in line with God's Word. Whenever you experience spiritual weariness, repeat the above prayer and Scripture verses. If you are spiritually or physically exhausted, take time for rest and renewal, then remind yourself of the experience of Moses in the case history that follows from the Word of God.

Prognosis:

Marvelous. Spiritual weariness can be relieved by addressing its underlying causes—natural fatigue from the spiritual and mental toll of ministering or taking too much responsibility on yourself. The first cause can be addressed by physical rest and downtime, prayer, fellowship with other believers, and reading God's Word. The second cause can be addressed by all of the above *and* by asking for the help of others for tasks that are too large to handle alone.

CASE HISTORY FROM THE WORD OF GOD:
Moses Judging the Israelites
(See Exodus 18:5–26.)

The Israelites who were traveling in the desert toward the Promised Land under Moses' leadership numbered approximately two million people. Imagine the logistics of coordinating that many people on the move! Then there was the additional need to govern the nation. Moses had always been the one to whom God had spoken His will, and so Moses sat as judge from morning until evening while the people brought him questions, complaints, and disputes for his counsel and ruling.

Moses had sent his wife and children to stay with his father-in-law Jethro while he attended to leading the people. At one point, however, Jethro felt the separation had been too lengthy, and so he escorted Moses' wife and family to where the Israelites were staying in the desert. Moses told Jethro everything God had done for His people, and Jethro praised God for His deliverance of the Israelites. After this reunion, Jethro observed Moses' method of judging the people, and he could see that it was an exhausting ordeal both for Moses and the people who stood for hours before

TAKE TIME FOR RENEWAL.

being able to see him. When he asked Moses about it, Moses explained that he needed to instruct the people in the ways of God. Jethro replied that his motivation was good and right, but that his method was impractical and even physically and mentally harmful. He suggested that Moses appoint godly men as rulers over smaller groups of people. These rulers could handle the less important issues, under Moses' guidance, and Moses could handle the larger issues. Moses wisely listened to his father-in-law's good counsel and was no longer burdened with unnecessary tasks. He had begun to think he was indispensable, but God was not asking him to do more than he could handle. Likewise, you should allow others to help you in the tasks that God has called you to do, instead of feeling as if you are the only one who can do them and then becoming overwhelmed.

7

Long-Term Health Plan
Spiritual Strength, Stamina, and Vitality

I was about to be released from the hospital, but I was in for a big surprise. The doctor had told me that I would need to use a wheelchair to help me get to my car, not just because this was hospital policy, but because I would be too weak to walk. "That's ridiculous," I thought. "I am simply going to get up and walk out of this hospital." But when I finally did get up from my bed, I had to sit right back down again. I was shocked at how weak I felt. The ordeal of my illness and the toll of the medical tests, such as the spinal taps, had depleted my strength. In addition, although lying immobile for ten days had been necessary for my overall healing, it had also caused my muscles to become weak and lose some of their flexibility. My illness was under control, and I was on the road to recovery. However, I would still need to rebuild my strength, and I would need to continue taking medication for a while, before I could return to my normal routine. My long-term prognosis for a healthy life also included continuing the good health habits I had already been practicing, so that my immune system could remain strong to combat further illnesses.

LIFELONG COMMITMENT

In a similar way, spiritual disciplines and "exercises" will help you to regain and maintain your spiritual health. Even after you have taken the prescription of God's *strong medicine* for your specific difficulty, and His grace and power have set you on the road to recovery, you can't just throw away the "medicine bottle" and go back to the way you had been living. If you were to suffer a heart attack and receive life-saving medical help, you could not return to eating a high-fat diet, smoking, or participating in other activities that put stress on the heart. You would need to practice a healthy lifestyle, including good nutrition and regular exercise. You might also need to take medicine on a long-term basis. Likewise, a crisis or trial can make you stronger, better able to persevere, and more spiritually alive because, in the long run, it causes you to focus on the essential practices and principles of a healthy spiritual life.

Our Great Physician has provided us with endless refills of His *strong medicine* for the many challenges we will continue to face and for our ongoing need for spiritual growth and maturity. Remaining spiritually healthy requires a *long-term spiritual health plan* and a *lifelong commitment to spiritual health* in which our lives are increasingly conformed to the image of Jesus Christ.

STARTING POINT

What God teaches you about His truth and His will through your adversities can be used as a starting point for beginning your long-term spiritual health plan. For instance, the day I left the hospital, I was very weak physically, but I was fully aware of what God was teaching me through my illness. Coming close to death and having to depend fully on God and others to provide for all my needs gave me a new level of compassion for people and helped me

ADVERSITY IS A STARTING POINT FOR MINISTRY.

see people through Jesus' eyes. I had to experience weakness so that I could understand and empathize with the weaknesses of others. This new understanding became the starting point for a new direction in my life, as God increased my ministry to people needing spiritual critical care. I would not be able to minister to them as effectively as I am able to today if I had not undergone trials in my life such as my illness. I am now able to minister to my congregations with a deeper level of compassion, and I am better able reach out to those who do not yet know Christ.

Like the man born blind whose story is recorded in John 9, I now understand that many of my past struggles were not the result of any fault of my own, but were permitted in my life by God to fulfill His greater purpose—providing ministry to change the lives of thousands for Christ across the world. My struggles were the training ground that God used to prepare and teach me, and to bring me to a greater level of maturity in Him. As a result, I have a level of compassion for hurting people that more closely resembles that of our Lord Jesus Christ than I had before. As you look back over your life, can you point to a problem that sent you running to God and, as a result, caused you to dig deeper and grow stronger in Him? Ultimately, that is what *successful living* is all about.

In a time when believers are experiencing many devastating personal and spiritual problems, we need people in the body of Christ who have a high level of understanding of such difficulties and who are not inclined to blame or condemn people who struggle with them. Those who have been through various trials themselves are especially sensitive to others in the body who are hurting, such as single parents or those who have gone through divorce or illness. People need someone they can go to who can minister the love and forgiveness of God and help them get on the road to restoration and recovery—in spite of their past difficulties.

Therefore, as you begin to put into place a long-term spiritual health plan, the first thing you should do is reflect on what God has taught you through your difficulty and how you can apply it to both your own life and your ministry to others. Use it as a starting point of obedience to God and of fulfilling His purposes for your life.

Second, you need to plan on adequate "recovery" time. When you apply God's *strong medicine* to a specific difficulty, you may immediately feel help and relief. Yet don't be discouraged if you still have to spend time regaining your spiritual strength, as I had to regain my physical strength after my illness. Your *"inner man"* will be strengthened by God's Spirit continually (Ephesians 3:16) as you make the commitment to lifelong spiritual health.

Third, a spiritual health plan requires an investment in resources for spiritual growth. This chapter outlines key areas that will enable you to complete your healing, develop good spiritual health habits, and fortify your spiritual immune system. These areas are *spiritual strength*—growing strong in the Lord; *spiritual stamina*—building spiritual muscles; and *spiritual vitality*—living the abundant life.

SPIRITUAL STRENGTH: GROWING STRONG IN THE LORD

The following are the most important spiritual health habits you can practice in order to grow strong in the Lord: being a lifelong student of the Word of God, maintaining an effective prayer life, and participating in the ministry of the body of Christ.

Being a Lifelong Student of the Word

For Transformation

The Bible is more than human theories or ideas; it is God's truth. The Scriptures

> *are able to make you wise for salvation through faith which is in Christ Jesus. All Scripture is given by inspiration of God, and is profitable for doctrine, for reproof, for correction, for instruction in righteousness, that the man [woman] of God may be complete, thoroughly equipped for every good work.*
> (2 Timothy 3:15–17)

The purpose of reading and studying the Bible is not just for your information but also for your transformation into the image of Christ, and this is a lifelong process. Becoming a believer and growing in Christ is not like trying to "turn over a new leaf" or making a New Year's resolution to change. It involves a transformation of your entire person, direction, outlook, and behavior. When you continually take in the *strong medicine* of the Word of God and apply it to your life, that crucial transformation can take place.

For Wisdom

You need to be a student of the Word of God in order to gain wisdom as well as transformation. Life on this earth is short, and if you are to live a successful life, you will need much greater wisdom than this confused and fallen world

185

can offer. You will need God's wisdom. If you listen to Him, His truth will spare you the bitterness of foolish choices. Dangers and uncertainties abound in life. True wisdom is seeing life from God's perspective and, therefore, knowing the best course of action to take. Even when your life experiences do not turn out the way you had hoped, you can be assured that wise living always produces a good outcome. We suffer unnecessary distress of every type in our lives when we fail to make use of the wisdom found in the Scriptures.

For Standing Fast

When I was in the hospital, and God warned me of Satan's plans to sabotage the work He wanted to do in my life, my key defense against the enemy was my knowledge of the Word of God—which Paul called *"the sword of the Spirit"* (Ephesians 6:17). The reason I was able to use the Sword is that I had trained myself in it and could apply it directly to my circumstances. God's promises are true, but you have to apply them—and you have to *know* them before you can apply them. You need to have the Sword with you (within your heart and mind) at all times, like a battle-ready soldier. Then you will be able to protect yourself against the attacks of the enemy.

THE WORD IS A KEY DEFENSE.

For Eternity

We frequently do not want to put forth the effort or commitment required to take regular doses of the medicine of the Word. Moreover, this *strong medicine* often works over time rather than instantaneously. Yet even though it may work slowly, in the long run, it is incomparable to all other substitutes for it. Moreover, its results last for a lifetime—and into eternity.

Maintaining an Effective Prayer Life

For Intimacy

The most important reason to pray is to develop an intimate relationship with your heavenly Father. God doesn't want any wall of separation between Him and you. In fact,

He will do everything possible to remove the things that separate you from Him or keep Him hidden from you. He doesn't want just "visiting hours" with His children. He wants to be a permanent resident in your life. *"If anyone loves Me, he will keep My word; and My Father will love him, and We will come to him and make Our home with him"* (John 14:23). Prayer can keep us in constant contact and fellowship with God.

For Addressing Specific Needs

Do you often find yourself praying "generic" prayers, such as "Lord, bless everyone and everything"? I think all of us have done that at times. However, when you truly seek God in prayer, when you really want answers from Him, your prayers should be specific. They should clearly address the area, in your life or in the lives of those for whom you are praying, that needs to be healed, forgiven, helped, or restored. Since God's *strong medicine* is specific to our individual concerns, He wants us to make these concerns known to Him so that He can provide specific healing prescriptions for us.

For Receiving Grace and Power

Prayer is essential to your long-term spiritual health because, in a very real way, God gives you His grace and power when you pray. He lightens your heavy heart, fills you with His peace, and gives you His strength, so that you can move forward in your life with a renewed sense of hope and purpose. Prayer is an incredible resource that enables you to live a joyful life and to serve the Lord with your whole being.

Participating in the Ministry of the Body

Another spiritual health habit for growing strong in the Lord is participating in the ministry of the body of Christ. By participation, I mean both receiving and serving—receiving the teaching, preaching, and encouragement of your spiritual leaders, and serving God with the gifts and talents that He has given you.

As an "Assisted Living Center"

An assisted living center is a place where a person who needs a degree of medical assistance on a regular basis can maintain independent living while enjoying the benefits of physical care and emotional support. The church is much like an assisted living center. While each believer has an individual relationship with God, if he or she becomes isolated from other believers, there is a risk of spiritual stagnation or decline. To maintain long-term spiritual health, you need to make use of the spiritual health benefits regularly available through the church: solid instruction in the Word of God by a mature Christian leader and fellowship and mutual encouragement from other believers.

When my father was diagnosed with cancer, he needed special assistance on a daily basis, but he did not want to feel dependent on his family for help. The best solution was for him to live in an assisted living facility, and I set about finding the best facility possible. The search was tedious and time-consuming, but it was very much worth the effort. The facility I found was clean and well-maintained. The staff was well-trained, experienced, and friendly. I felt confident that my father would receive the quality care he needed. In the same way, we should exercise diligence when looking for a church that can provide us with the spiritual care and support we need. Sometimes such a search can be painstaking and time-consuming, but it will be worthwhile, because the degree to which we grow as Christians will be influenced by the person or persons who exercise spiritual care over us.

It is your responsibility to find a church where you can grow and learn. You need to ask God to direct you to a church that is Word-centered, where there is an emphasis on solid Bible teaching, and where you will be taught how to apply the Word to your life. When I was looking for an assisted living facility for my father, I was searching for the *right* place for him and his needs, not just a place that was immediately available and inexpensive. My goal was to find the very best care for him. Likewise, your goal as a Christian should be to seek out the right church that will enable you to grow and maintain maximum spiritual health.

SEEK OUT THE RIGHT CHURCH.

As a Crisis Response Center

A crisis response center is a facility for people who are undergoing physical, psychological, or emotional problems that are not so severe that they need to go to a hospital, but are serious enough that they need professional intervention. Crisis response centers are located within local communities so that they can be easily accessed. They are equipped to address a variety of medical, physical, and emotional needs from which people in the community might suffer.

Likewise, the church is to be like a crisis response center—available to the community to assist in personal crises. When a member of the church or surrounding community suffers a spiritual, emotional, or physical trauma, a prepared and equipped church family will be able to immediately respond to their needs in a Christlike way. You need to assess and use the spiritual gifts and talents that God has given you, so that you can respond to others who are experiencing crises in their lives with the love of Christ.

As a "Paramedic"

Paramedics do not have the same training, knowledge, or skills that physicians have, but they perform a vital role in the medical community. Their job is to stabilize patients until a physician can attend to them. "Paramedics" in the church are its pastors, teachers, and intercessors who assist Christ, the Great Physician. If you serve in such a role, your job is to help "stabilize" believers in their faith by showing them how to apply God's strong medicine to their lives, giving them spiritual guidance, and nurturing their growth in the Lord. You are not the Medical Doctor, and you do not bring the actual healing. However, you have a crucial role in bringing Christians to Christ the Healer, so that He can minister to them.

STAMINA: BUILDING SPIRITUAL MUSCLES

Through a Spiritual Maintenance Plan

An important part of your recovery and growth process will be to strengthen your spiritual "muscles" so that you can build stamina in the Lord. Sometimes we are shocked when, long after we thought we had gained complete victory in an area of weakness in our lives, we find ourselves having slipped back into an old sinful habit. Many times, Christians can become very deeply depressed when this happens because they thought they had been delivered from sin. However, we need not only to be delivered from sin, but also to *maintain* that deliverance so that we can truly be set free from sinful habits and practices in our lives.

Jesus told a parable about a man who was delivered from a demon, whose life was "swept" clean and put in order. Yet because the man did not fill his life with the Spirit and the Word of God, the demon came back with seven other demons that were more wicked than he was. They inhabited the man again, and he ended up in a worse state than he had been before. (See Matthew 12:43–45.)

Sometimes people who know they have been delivered from promiscuity, homosexuality, or addiction, but who are then tempted to fall back into these behaviors, come to me and ask, "What should I do?" I say to them, "It is your responsibility to maintain an intimate relationship with the Lord and to establish healthy relationships with strong Christians in order to maintain your deliverance." I emphasize that even when they are *tempted* by those old attractions, they must not *engage* in the sinful behaviors. We must remember that the sin is not in the thoughts that continue to tempt us. but in our yielding to those thoughts and in returning to those old behaviors.

HAVE A PLAN IN PLACE.

You are delivered from your sins when you sincerely confess to God and repent with godly sorrow. However, you will be truly set free as you continue to maintain that deliverance through a close relationship with the Lord and through allowing the *strong medicine* of the Word of God to work in your life on a long-term basis. You must take God's prescribed medicine over a period of a lifetime for it to continue to be effective. It cannot be just a temporary thing that you do. For example, I love decorating, and I did some decorating in my office that included a lot of personal touches. When I was finished, I felt it looked picture perfect. However, if I did not have a maintenance plan in place for cleaning, vacuuming, polishing, and touching up here and there on a weekly or monthly basis, then in thirty to sixty days, that beautiful room would begin to collect dust and deteriorate.

Over a very short period of time, it would be an unkempt, uninviting room.

It is the same way in our spiritual lives. We can start out strong in the things of God, yet our spiritual vitality can decline, not only as a result of blatant sin or turning away from God, but also as a result of not having a serious spiritual maintenance plan in place. Just as dust and neglect make a room look unkempt, we can become "unkempt" in areas of our lives if we do not purpose to maintain these areas through reading the Word of God, spending time with Him in prayer, and fellowshipping with other believers.

Through "Quarantine"

Another way you can maintain your spiritual muscles is by "quarantining" yourself against "contagious" spiritual diseases. You wouldn't go into a person's hospital room if you knew that person had a highly infectious disease. Similarly, especially if you are a new Christian, your life should be in a kind of "quarantine," because light has no fellowship with darkness (2 Corinthians 6:14 NIV). If you hang around in places where you can be easily infected or re-infected with sinful behavior, then you are risking your spiritual health. You have to actively watch over your own life and behavior—where you go and what you do.

A person can develop an illness and not realize it for three or four days. What starts out as a minor cough can end up as pneumonia if a person does not take the proper care. Likewise, we have to live clean, pure lives before God at all times to avoid being "infected." We cannot live a little bit in Christ and a little bit in the filth of the world and expect to stay healthy. We are to be the light of the world and reach out to others with Christ's love, but we have to make sure that we are not drawn back into the world. Just as a diseased organ, such as an infected appendix, must be removed from the body through surgery, so that it will not cause further medical problems, there are times when you will have to remove "toxic" people and situations from your life so that they will not cause you further spiritual problems. You will have to remove yourself from negative situations where ungodly things are going on to which you are susceptible.

Compounding the problem is the fact that we are often drawn to others who have underlying issues in their lives that are similar to the ones with which we struggle. For example, people who are not emotionally healthy tend to be drawn to and get involved in relationships with others who have the same kinds of problems. I once heard a psychologist say that we tend to run *to* what we think we are running *from*. For example, if you have issues of abandonment in your family system, you will probably be drawn to people who struggle with the same issue. Then you might wonder why you go from one person to the next, never being able to enter into a stable relationship. It will take a certain vigilance over your life to keep yourself spiritual healthy.

Through "Spiritual Autopsies"

Examining underlying issues and root causes of problems in your family system is like performing a "spiritual autopsy." When a coroner performs an autopsy on a cadaver, she discovers a wealth of information. An autopsy can reveal the cause of death, as well as a person's general lifestyle and health habits.

Likewise, there are certain issues and destructive patterns of behavior in our lives that have been passed down to us in our families. Some of these issues have been so serious that they have caused "deathlike" consequences in our relationships with other people. An excellent way to build spiritual muscle is to learn from the past, to do "spiritual autopsies" on past attitudes and trials in our lives. An autopsy is performed by a knowledgeable medical examiner or pathologist, and often, when we finally examine painful issues in our lives, we can benefit from talking to a pastoral counselor who is knowledgeable in the things of God. A mature pastoral counselor acts like a "spiritual coroner" in helping us to examine underlying issues of pathological behavior and root causes of problems in our family systems. In our spiritual lives, we need to go back and look at certain hurts and family patterns that will help us to understand

UNRESOLVED ISSUES CAN BE "SILENT KILLERS."

more about behaviors and patterns in our lives that we need to address.

When we take a look at prior problems that we haven't handled correctly and analyze the "death" that they have caused and the extent of deterioration they have produced, we can avoid these problems in the future in order to remain spiritually healthy. We will sometimes discover that problems and issues have been building within us for years. We never addressed them, but the damage was so great that it was like a silent killer. Some diseases—such as tumors—can grow inside the body for years. However, a person might not be aware of the presence of the tumor until the pain becomes so excruciating that it sends the person running to a doctor. Sometimes, we know something is not quite right in our lives, but we don't do anything about it. It takes time and effort to examine something that might cause us emotional pain. It is easier to just continue going along as we have been—until we make enough mistakes in certain areas of our lives that the emotional pain is so great it causes us to stop and say, "I'd better address this, or it will kill me."

Through Godly Living

Finally, two powerful forces that will enable you to build spiritual muscles are godliness and integrity. The psalmist asked God to give him these qualities as "bodyguards" to protect him in his life. *"Let integrity and uprightness preserve me, for I wait for You"* (Psalm 25:21).

True *godliness* is total dependence on Christ and His righteousness. It protects you from thinking you can fight life's battles alone or seek entrance to your eternal home on your own merits. It causes you to depend on God for His help. *Integrity* is living a consistent and honorable life before God. It is being in reality what you say you believe and what you say you are; this will keep you from claiming to be godly while living as if you do not know Him. Godliness says, "This is God's way," and integrity says, "I will walk consistently in it." Remember that acknowledging your weaknesses to God not only helps to develop Christian character in you, but also helps to deepen your worship, for in admitting your weaknesses, you affirm God's strength. When you feel that you are strong in your own abilities or resources, you will be tempted to do God's work on your own, and this will lead to pride. However, when you acknowledge that your own abilities and resources are inadequate, you allow God to fill you with His power. Then you will be stronger than you ever could have been on your own, and you will be able to live a consistent, godly life. You must depend on God, for only work done in His power has lasting value and will make you effective for Him.

VITALITY: LIVING THE ABUNDANT LIFE

The third key area of a long-term spiritual health plan is vitality. *Vitality* is the capacity to live, grow, and develop. Moreover, the definition of health is "the condition of being sound in body, mind, and spirit," "well-being," and "a flourishing condition." These definitions give us an indication of the vitality of life that God desires for us. There are several key ways in which we can enter into this abundant life.

Through Intimacy with the Lord

When I returned home after ten days in the hospital, I noticed that my skin was extremely clear, and I asked my doctor about this on a later visit. She said that when I was in the hospital, I had been properly hydrated and that, although I had been ill, my body had really *rested* for those ten days. Because I had been fed intravenously, my body had also experienced an inner cleansing. At the same time, I had received the optimum amount of vitamins and nutrients. All this good care was manifested in my physical appearance.

However, I think there was more to it than that. I believe that the deeper spiritual experience I had with the Lord during that time was also evidenced in my renewed physical appearance. When I had visitors, and when I was able to go out for short walks and day trips, people remarked that I looked different. I know that there was a spiritual as well as a physical reason for this difference. Since my crisis was such a turning point in my life, and my relationship with the Lord was deepened to such an extremely intimate level, the change became evident even in my physical countenance. When Moses was in the presence of the Lord, the experience was so powerful that his face shined with the glory of the Lord. When he came down from Mount Sinai, he had to put a cloth over his face because the light of God's glory was still emanating from it. I knew that the change in my countenance was due to a similar reason, because I was not the same person who had gone into that hospital. I had met the Lord "face-to-face."

When you have a vital relationship with the Lord, it will be evident to other people. In medicine, *vital signs* are signs of the existence of life, such as a beating heart, the breath of the body, and physical movement. In your spiritual life, you should have evident vital signs—signs that your relationship with the Lord is alive and well. Those signs are evident when you have a hunger and thirst for the Word of God; **SPIRITUAL VITALITY IS EVIDENT.** when you have a desire to grow; when you study and apply the Word to your life; when you exhibit the fruit of the Spirit; and when you are eager to fellowship with other Christians who love the Lord as you do.

When spiritual vital signs are not present in your life, you know that your spiritual health is in danger. There is a big difference between a living being and a corpse. You can see and touch a corpse, and it exists, but it is not alive, because there are no longer any signs of vitality. Similarly, you can sit in church, study the Word, and go through the motions, but when there are no signs of spiritual life in you, because you have not applied the Word to your life, then you lack spiritual vitality.

However, God can renew His life within you. A person might receive a blood transfusion to compensate for losing too much blood; similarly, Jesus' blood will cleanse you when your spiritual health has been depleted due to sin. When certain hormones are out of balance in a person's body, the person can take medicine to regulate them—such as medicine that increases a low thyroid level. Likewise, the Word of God can bring you back into "spiritual balance" when you have moved away from a close relationship with the Lord.

Through Our Perspective on Adversity

It is not what happens to you but it is how you *react* to what happens to you and what you learn from it that is important. Medically, when a person has a cheerful and optimistic outlook, he or she can recover from illness faster than someone who has a pessimistic attitude. In fact, laughter is used as a treatment plan in some hospitals and nursing homes.

We cannot control how Satan will attack us, but we can choose how we will respond when it happens. The familiar verse from Proverbs, *"A merry heart does good, like medicine"* (Proverbs 17:22) is applicable to both physical and spiritual prognoses. We will receive strength and refreshing when we are filled with the joy of the Lord (Nehemiah 8:10) and can praise Him no matter what the circumstances.

Through Trusting in Our Policyholder

Most of us have insurance so that we will be cared and provided for if we suffer illnesses or accidents. However, *all* of us as believers have spiritual *assurances* from God. Jesus is the Policyholder of all our "spiritual assurance policies." He gives us complete assurance coverage: health, whole life, accident, catastrophic loss, and "hellfire" protection. As children of God, we are His "dependents." We can be assured that He will never default on His premium payments, because He has already paid the full price with His blood on Calvary.

God gives us His assurances mainly through the Scripture, so that, if we are built up and prepared by the Word, when adversity comes along, we will not be caught off guard by it. If you see someone on the news whose house has burned down but no one was killed, and the person is very calm, it probably means that she has insurance. But if you see someone who is hysterical, it is because he knows his whole life has gone up in smoke. He was totally unprepared. From day to day, we don't know what is going to happen to us, and that is why we need to have life and health insurance. Likewise, in our spiritual lives, we need to

GOD HAS AN "ASSURANCE" PLAN.

depend on the assurances of God. We do this by consistently developing an intimate relationship with Him before difficulty comes or tragedy strikes.

Through Having an Eternal Perspective

It is ironic that people spend so much time establishing their lives on earth but spend little or no time preparing for where they will spend eternity. Jesus challenges you to think beyond earthbound goals and to use what you have been given for God's kingdom. When you have a clear understanding from God's Word that each of us has a limited time on earth, you will change the way you have been living and take the time to confess your sins, receive forgiveness from God, and reexamine the direction of your life. Since all of us will eventually die, it makes sense for us to plan ahead so that we will experience God's mercy and live eternally with Him. Focusing on what is really important to your life on earth will help you retain much-needed spiritual vitality in your service for Christ.

The Daily Dosages that follow in the next chapter will help you apply what you have learned throughout this book to your specific circumstances, so that you can establish the practice of consistently using God's strong medicine during times of adversity. Through one month of reminding yourself of the truths and promises of God, and applying them to your circumstances, you will be well on your way to developing a long-term spiritual health plan for your life.

8
DAILY DOSAGES
Take As Directed

This final chapter includes a full month of daily dosages of God's *strong medicine*. Each dosage has been specifically designed for your spiritual encouragement and growth. It will take you just fifteen to thirty minutes a day to read and reflect on each dosage. The spiritual benefits of following this plan will be well worth the investment of your time and reflection. Experts claim that it takes a person about twenty-one days to form a habit—good or bad. This program gives you even better than that—four weeks of daily dosages—so that you can make the development of your spiritual growth a consistent habit as you establish a lifelong spiritual health plan and reap its eternal benefits.

DIRECTIONS FOR USAGE

As you apply these daily dosages to your life, you will experience times of refreshment, reflection, renewal, and accelerated growth. After each group of seven dosages, or each week, you will also have an opportunity for further reflection and spiritual exercises by using the journal spaces provided. God gives us an opportunity to partner with Him in our spiritual growth. However, as with any good medical procedure, the full cooperation of the patient is necessary if the care that is offered is to be successful. Trust the Holy Spirit to deepen your relationship with the Lord and to help you develop godly habits as you respond to His guidance and instruction each day.

INDICATIONS

You may take these daily dosages during your quiet times with the Lord or with others in a Bible study or prayer group. Remember that the Word of God will only be acquired knowledge to you and will not work effectively until it is applied to the area of your trauma or hurt. Then it can directly address your situation and bring about healing.

Here are some helpful guidelines to follow as you apply these daily dosages, or **P-I-L-L-S**, of God's strong medicine to your life:

P   *Pray.*

I   *Identify* an area of concern in your life.

L   *Learn* what the Word of God says about your situation.

L   *Live* in the truth of God's promises to you.

S   *Strengthen* your commitment to lifelong spiritual health as you are healed by the application of the Word to your life.

As you follow this plan, my prayer is that you will experience the presence of God in such a liberating way that you will delight in trusting Him as He lifts you above life's traumas and draws you to Himself in love, compassion, and healing.

Week 1: Acknowledge Your Difficulties

Day 1
Scripture Reading: Psalm 25

The first step in receiving God's *strong medicine* is to acknowledge your pain to God. He has deep compassion for you and wants to help you in the midst of your adversities. Take a few moments today to think about a problem that has been troubling you for some time or a trauma you have just experienced. Express your pain and bewilderment to God. Ask Him to come into your situation today and to begin to use it for your good and His glory.

Day 2
Scripture Reading: Philippians 4:11–13

Life can change in a moment—for the bad or the good. Someone you love is in a car accident. You get a bonus in your paycheck. A routine exam reveals a serious condition. Your son receives a scholarship to college. If your emotional and spiritual security depend on circumstances, you will likely live a roller-coaster existence instead of in the power, love, and soundness of mind God offers you (2 Timothy 1:7). Make a commitment today to anchor your life in the One who will keep you in *"perfect peace"* (Isaiah 26:3)—despite life's ups and downs.

Day 3
Scripture Reading: James 1:2–4

Your most valuable life lessons, the ones that best prepare you to reach up to God and to reach out to others, will be those that are learned through "impossible" situations, because God's strength is made perfect through your weaknesses. During these times, when you ask God the right questions, you allow Him the opportunity to give you the answers you need in order to grow. As you pray about your struggles, instead of asking, "Why me, Lord?" ask:

What are You trying to tell me, God?
Lord, what am I to learn in this?
God, what direction do You want me to take?

Day 4
Scripture Reading: Ephesians 6:11–18
Don't be surprised by the devil's attacks on your life. Discouragement, evil thoughts, trials—these tactics come naturally to him. However, Satan's wicked ploys are no match for the armor of God. Remember whose side you are on: Jesus is the Victor! Put on the full armor of God today.

Day 5
Scripture Reading: Psalm 131
The pace of our lifestyles and the up-to-the-minute technology we use to keep in touch with others—cell phones, E-mail, pagers—make it difficult for us to find time to be alone with God. Make a commitment to spend quiet time with God on a regular basis, so that you can hear His *still small voice* (1 Kings 19:12) and receive His guidance, strength, and encouragement for your life.

Day 6
Scripture Reading: Lamentations 3:22–25
Take a few minutes now to remember and thank God for helping you through difficult times when you weren't sure you would make it, but did—in His strength. His compassion never fails; His faithfulness is great. His mercy is new each day. He has helped you in the past, and He will help you in your current situation.

Day 7
Scripture Reading: Psalm 121
If you are in need of intensive, round-the-clock care, the Scripture reading for today will encourage you that the Great Physician is always on duty. He never sleeps, never takes a break, never turns His patients over to someone else's charge. Rest in His care today, and allow Him to administer His healing and comfort to you. Use the journal opportunity for this week to identify the underlying cause of your difficulty.

Daily Dosages Journal for Week 1
Analyze the Cause

Making a spiritual diagnosis of your difficulty is an essential step in applying God's *strong medicine* to it. Yet only by relying on the guidance of the Holy Spirit can you arrive at an accurate diagnosis. After you read the Scripture and pray the prayer below, write about a difficulty in your life, its symptoms and how you are responding to it, and what might be the source of your trial. Take time to carefully consider your problem through prayer and reading God's Word. Remember that the major sources of your trials are (1) the temptations of the world; (2) the lusts of your own carnal nature; (3) the wiles of the devil; (4) the persecution that believers of the Lord Jesus Christ undergo as His followers; and (5) the temporary removal of God's hedge of protection for His glory and your greater good.

Scripture Readings: Hebrews 4:12; Psalm 139:23–24
Prayer for a Yielded Heart:
Lord, help me to understand the nature of my difficulty. Enable me to distinguish Your voice from my own thoughts and the deception of the enemy. Thank you for Your guidance. In Jesus' name, Amen.

My difficulty is...

_____

_____

_____

_____

The symptoms of my difficulty are...

_____

_____

_____

_____

I am responding to my symptoms by...

_____

_____

_____

_____

After prayer and reading God's Word, I believe the source of my difficulty is...

_____

_____

Now that you have read God's word, prayed, and considered the cause of your difficulty, write down anything you feel God is showing you about it. Don't hurry the process, but keep seeking God until you receive His guidance regarding the source of your problem. Discuss your conclusions with a trusted friend or pastoral counselor.

_____

_____

_____

_____

_____

_____

_____

Prayer of Commitment:
Dear Lord, thank You for giving me Your wisdom to understand my situation in the light and truth of Your Word. Grant me a willing spirit so that I will respond in obedience to what You reveal to me about my circumstance. Amen.

Week 2: Address Your Difficulties

Day 8

Scripture Readings: Luke 1:37; Ephesians 1:18–23

It is almost comical to envision David slaying Goliath with just a slingshot and a stone. However, you should never underestimate the power of your God-given resources. No matter how insignificant they may appear, His limitless power is at work in them—and through you. Ask God to enable you to rely on His resources during your trial, so that you may receive His strength, courage, and victory.

Day 9

Scripture Readings: Colossians 1:10–12; James 5:10–11

Usually, having too much patience isn't our problem. We want answers, and we want them yesterday! If you are feeling impatient, submit to God's timing, and praise Him in the midst of your difficulty. Lessons learned while waiting are worth waiting for.

Day 10

Scripture Reading: Romans 5:3–5

When people look on suffering as something to avoid, this view can lead to physical ailments, depression, addiction, and even suicide. Yet God sees our sufferings as an opportunity to conform us to His image, increase our dependence on Him, and enable us to comfort others with the comfort He has shown to us. Your view of suffering can either lead you to further distress or to hope in Christ. Which view of suffering do you have?

Day 11

Scripture Reading: Joshua 1:8–9

Doctors advise patients against the tendency to stop taking their medication at the first sign of returning health. Likewise, you should avoid neglecting spiritual disciplines, such as reading your Bible, praying, and fellowshipping with other Christians, once you start to feel an easing of your symptoms of distress. Remember to take *all* of the *strong medicine* God has prescribed.

Day 12
Scripture Reading: Jeremiah 29:11–13

Exchange the worries of today and the uncertainties of tomorrow for God's encouraging, assuring prognosis for your future. Whenever you find yourself thinking in a negative way:

➢ Practice listening to yourself, noting the number of fearful and negative remarks you make.
➢ Ask yourself, "Do I really believe what I am saying, or am I speaking negativism out of habit?"
➢ Put the best connotation on the words and actions of every person and on every situation.
➢ Keep track of everything that happens as you practice this new procedure. Carefully note even the smallest positive results.

Day 13
Scripture Reading: 1 Peter 1:3–4

Take a few minutes to read through the Bible promises at the end of chapters 1–5 of this book. Let God's words enter your mind and settle in your heart. Then rest in His great love for you.

Day 14
Scripture Reading: Luke 4:14–18

Just as physical pain can serve as a warning of a serious health problem, emotional pain can be a sign of spiritual illness that needs your immediate attention. If you are crippled by fear, paralyzed by low self-esteem, haunted by painful memories, or burdened by hopelessness, it is a good time to undergo a spiritual "examination." God wants to heal your broken heart and free you from your spiritual captivity. Turn to Him in prayer, saturate your mind with His Word, and seek out wise counselors who will offer you godly advice. Use the journal opportunity for this week to come to terms with your difficulty so that you can apply God's *strong medicine* to it.

DAILY DOSAGES JOURNAL FOR WEEK 2
Face the Problem

Accurately diagnosing your difficulty is a crucial step in the healing process, yet it is not a complete solution. You will need to *confront* your problem if you are to find healing and wholeness. Review chapter four and the various ways in which we can avoid dealing with painful circumstances in our lives. After you read the Scripture and pray the prayer below, write out ways in which you may have been using a "painkiller" to assuage your emotional pain rather than dealing with it directly.

Scripture Readings: 2 Chronicles 20:1–15; 1 Samuel 17:45–50
Prayer for a Yielded Heart:

Lord, help me to recognize and acknowledge the ways in which I have sought false painkillers to ease the pain of my adversity. Grant me the courage to face both my pain and the cause of it, knowing that the battle belongs to You, and that You will grant me the victory. Amen.

I have been using a "painkiller" to lessen my emotional pain by...

_____

_____

_____

_____

_____

_____

_____

_____

_____

_____

_____

Now that you have read God's word, prayed, and written down ways in which you have tried to avoid dealing with adversity, write down specific ways that you will trust God and use the resources He has given you to face your circumstance.

I will trust God in my difficulty by...

_____

_____

_____

_____

_____

I will use these resources God has given me in order to face my difficulty...

_____

_____

_____

_____

_____

_____

_____

_____

Prayer of Commitment:
Dear Lord, thank You for giving me Your wisdom, strength, and courage to face my situation in the light and truth of Your Word. Grant me a willing spirit so that I will respond in obedience to what You reveal about my situation and how I am to address it. Amen.

Week 3: Allow God to Use Your Trials for Good

Day 15

Scripture Reading: 2 Corinthians 4:16–18

God is more interested in changing *you* than in changing your circumstances. Are you cooperating with His efforts? Are you studying His Word, taking His *strong medicine,* and following His *prescriptions for successful living?* Obedience to His will and His plans for your life will lead to spiritual healing. Commit today to cooperate with Him fully in the healing process.

Day 16

Scripture Readings: Jeremiah 31:3; Proverbs 8:35; Ephesians 1:6

Do you consider yourself to be more like Leah than Rachel? Do you feel as if you are always second best? Reread today's Scripture readings, and receive God's truth about yourself. When you really know the truth, it sets you free to love and to be loved. Rejoice in God's love for you today.

Day 17

Scripture Readings: Galatians 6:9; 1 Peter 4:19

During her lifetime, Leah never knew that through her lineage Jesus Christ would be born. Your faithfulness to God today determines not only your eternal destiny but also your spiritual legacy.

Day 18

Scripture Reading: Philippians 3:7–15

Do you reverse the apostle Paul's advice by forgetting the things that are ahead and reaching toward the hurtful things in your past? Since Jesus has already forgiven you, accept His forgiveness and extend it to yourself. Rehearsing past mistakes is like constantly reopening a wound that is trying to heal. Allow the Great Physician to heal your wounds with His soothing balm. Thank Him today for setting you free so that you may look to your future with freedom and joy.

Day 19
Scripture Reading: Hebrews 12:11–15
What needs to be rooted out of your heart? Bitterness, jealousy, disappointment, shame, fear, anger, immorality? Only God can get to the root of your problems. Allow Him to loosen the hard soil of your heart. Fertilize your mind with His promises. Let the light and water of His Spirit saturate your soul. Then watch as the fruit of the Spirit blossoms forth in your life.

Day 20
Scripture Reading: Colossians 3:12–15
Everyone must enroll in the "school of forgiveness." It is a required course in the Christian life. Being angry at others and holding grudges against them requires your time, energy, and focus. It is stress-producing. Stress is inevitable, but stress-related illness is not. Learn to love others as Christ has loved you—even when you were "unlovable."

Day 21
Scripture Reading: Hebrews 11:1–16
Your life's journey will take you through many afflictions. Some people take up residence in the midst of their troubles and never leave them. Yet as God's child, you know you are just passing through this fallen world. You have an excellent spiritual prognosis for overcoming adversity as you keep your eyes on the goal: becoming like Christ on this earth and living with Him in eternity. Use the journal opportunity for this week to better understand how to maintain a good spiritual prognosis in the midst of adversity.

DAILY DOSAGES JOURNAL FOR WEEK 3
Believe the Promises

Once you have identified the cause of your adversity and have accepted God's strength to address it, it is important that you maintain your spiritual strength so that your prognosis for overcoming adversity will remain excellent. You can do this by holding tightly to the promises of God, sharing His perspective on adversity, and living in His plan and provision for your life. Keep in mind that God is interested in developing His character and ways in you, and that this goal is even more important than the adversities you go through. Remember that He has promised to be faithful to complete the work He has begun in you. After reading the Scripture and praying the prayer below, use the journal space provided to write about an area in your life that you feel God is asking you to work on, such as unforgiveness, fear, or selfishness. Entrust this area to God, knowing that He will change you as you yield to Him and trust His promises to make you into the image of His Son.

Scripture Readings: Romans 8:26–39; Hebrews 10:19–23
Prayer for a Yielded Heart:
Lord God, thank You for Your great and precious promises to me, especially Your promise to make me like Your Son. Please change the areas of my life that do not reflect Your goodness, grace, and power. I ask You to keep me spiritually strong as I yield my life to You, so that I will be able to address my adversities in Your strength and wisdom. In Jesus' name, Amen.

The main area I feel God wants me to work on in my life is...

_____

_____

_____

_____

_____

I will entrust this area to God by...

_____

_____

_____

_____

_____

   Now that you have read God's Word, prayed, and written about an area of your life that needs to be changed, write down Scriptures and promises in God's Word that relate to this area, and meditate on them during the next week.

Scriptures that relate to my area of difficulty are...

_____

_____

_____

_____

_____

_____

_____

_____

Prayer of Commitment:
Dear Lord, thank You for working in my life to make me more like Jesus as I go through adversity. Enable me to take to heart the Scriptures that correspond to the area You are calling me to change. I ask You to fill me afresh with Your Spirit so that there is no room in my heart for anything that is not of you. In Jesus' name, Amen.

Week 4: Maintain Your Spiritual Health

Day 22

Scripture Reading: Philippians 2:12–16

Making a good start is significant, but making a lifetime commitment is essential to achieving and maintaining both physical and spiritual health. When you are tempted to return to bad habits or to neglect good ones, ask God to help you to continue on a disciplined path. Each success will bring you closer to your ultimate goal.

Day 23

Scripture Reading: James 1:5–16

Once we recover from an illness, it is easy to forget how sick we were. Through careless living, we can expose ourselves to the same circumstances that led to illness in the first place. Likewise, we must be careful to maintain spiritual purity in order to be strong in the Lord. Are there people or places you are allowing yourself to have contact with that are causing you to become spiritually weak? Ask God for wisdom and strength to avoid harmful influences and to live a holy life.

Day 24

Scripture Readings: 1 Corinthians 16:13–14; 1 John 2:14–17

You should be exhibiting spiritual "vital signs"— signs that your relationship with the Lord is alive and well. Check your vital signs:

➤ Do you have a hunger and thirst for the Word of God?
➤ Do you have a desire to grow spiritually?
➤ Do you study and apply the Word of God to your life?
➤ Are you exhibiting the fruit of the Spirit?
➤ Are you eager to fellowship with other Christians who love the Lord?

If your vital signs are weak, ask God to renew them in your life; then make extra time to saturate your mind and heart with the Word of God.

Day 25
Scripture Reading: Psalm 103

Having an ongoing intimate relationship with the Lord will keep you spiritually healthy. Spend time today praising, worshipping, and thanking Him for who He is and what He has done for you.

Day 26
Scripture Reading: Matthew 6:19–24

Think about what you value in your life—where you place your time, energy, and money. To use Solomon's words in Ecclesiastes, will you one day look back and decide that these things were a "chasing after the wind"? This is a hard question to ask yourself, but the answer is crucial to your spiritual life. If you live with an eternal perspective in mind, you will be spiritually strong and healthy. Ask God to enable you to keep His goals and His will foremost in your life.

Day 27
Scripture Reading: 2 Corinthians 1:3–7

How encouraging it is to realize that God redeems the hard times we have gone through! When you are surrendered to Him, He will use you to minister to others. Your mended heart will become powerful medicine for someone else's broken spirit. Allow God to transform your former pain into a balm for a hurting soul.

Day 28
Scripture Reading: Ephesians 5:15–17

Have you developed a long-term spiritual health plan for your life? What books of the Bible will you study? What Scriptures will you memorize? Will you set aside time for prayer and getting to know the voice of God? What areas of your life will you ask God to change? With whom will you reconcile? Will you ask God to use you in ministering to others? Don't delay in making a plan for your spiritual growth—because life passes quickly. After praying about and thinking through the above questions, use the journal opportunity for this week to start developing a spiritual health plan for your life.

DAILY DOSAGES JOURNAL FOR WEEK 4
Lifelong Spiritual Health

You might ask, "Is there life after adversity?" A full spiritual life is available to you before, during, and after adversity. The key is to remain spiritually strong in both the "good" and the "bad" times. By living in God's ways and purposes, you can remain strong in the Lord, equipped for anything He calls you to do. Many Christians don't associate *planning* with their spiritual lives because we are to be led by God's Spirit (Romans 8:14). While it is true that we must be led by the Spirit, we are also to be wise in planning for our lives and the future. The Bible tells us to *study* to show ourselves approved (2 Timothy 2:15 KJV). It also says we are to be diligent to make our calling and election sure (2 Peter 1:10). We need to take action rather than expect our spiritual growth to come automatically. After you read the Scripture and pray the prayer below, begin to write out a long-term spiritual health plan for your life in each area listed. Seek the Holy Spirit's direction as you plan for spiritual growth.

Scripture Readings: 2 Timothy 2:11–15; 2 Peter 3:1–18

Prayer for a Yielded Heart:

Lord God, thank You for providing me with so many resources to bring me back to spiritual health and to keep me strong in You. I ask You to give me a hunger and thirst for righteousness, so that I will actively carry out a plan for my spiritual growth and well-being. As I am led by Your Spirit, let me be diligent to grow in the grace and knowledge of Jesus. Amen.

In order to study and memorize the Bible, I plan to...

_____

_____

_____

_____

In order to deepen my prayer life, I plan to...

_____

_____

_____

_____

Daily Dosages

In order to grow in the fruit of the Spirit, I plan to...

_____

_____

_____

_____

In order to forgive and reconcile with others, I plan to...

_____

_____

_____

_____

In order to minister to others, I plan to...

_____

_____

_____

_____

Prayer of Commitment:

Dear Lord, thank You for working in my life to make me more like Jesus. Enable me to grow spiritually strong and healthy by applying the resources You have given me through Your Spirit, Your Word, prayer, and ministering to others. Let me make the most of my time and stay close to You, because life is short. The days in which I am living are filled with temptations to fall away from You, and there are so many obstacles to loving You. For your sake, let me love You with all my heart, soul, mind, and strength. In Jesus' name, Amen.

Follow-Up Visit

Have you come to the place where you are able to think of adverse circumstances as blessings when God is involved in them? There are no wasted events in your life. Every situation and trial you experience has been allowed by God for a purpose. As you trust in Him, He will redeem your difficulties, using them to make you more like Jesus and enabling you to better understand Him and His ways.

After being discharged from the hospital, I went to the doctor for a follow-up visit. I asked her if I ever had to worry about getting spinal meningitis again. I wanted to know if my body had built up an immunity to the disease, as is possible with other illnesses. For example, if you get chicken pox or the measles, the chances are good that you will never contract either disease again. However, my doctor told me that spinal meningitis is the type of disease to which one cannot build an immunity, and that there are no guarantees that I will never contract it again.

That knowledge made me sad; however, I became encouraged when I realized that I now had an advantage from already having had the experience of undergoing the illness. I am now equipped with information, knowledge, and experience regarding spinal meningitis, and I know its symptoms: fatigue, a sore neck, and an excruciating headache that a pain reliever will not easily alleviate. If I were ever to have these symptoms, I would know that I would have to go to the emergency room immediately. Having spinal meningitis made me aware of the disease and its characteristics and symptoms; now I can be alert to the signs of its presence in myself and others. I am much better prepared to respond to it than I was before my intensive care experience, when I attributed my headache to other factors.

Likewise, the Bible does not guarantee that you will never face struggles again after you have gone through a trial, as if you can build an immunity to experiencing trials. Remember that *"many are the afflictions of the righteous, but the LORD delivers him* [her] *out of them all"* (Psalm 34:19). When you have already gone through a trial, and have received God's *strong medicine* for overcoming it, you have a powerful spiritual advantage for the next trial: you now know to go to God immediately with your difficulty and to trust Him to use it for your good; you know you can evaluate its signs and symptoms, with God's guidance, to determine its cause; and you have learned to use the resources God has given you to win victory over it.

Some of the hurts that we receive are only minor in nature. They amount to nothing more than day-to-day bruises and need to be brushed aside as quickly as they arise. These are hurts that have not been inflicted intentionally—like a careless word or an embarrassing remark made by a friend. Certain hurts are going to come our way in the normal course of daily living. It is the price we pay for being alive. These kinds of hurts should require nothing more than a "bandage" and a little time to heal. There is no point in making a mountain out of a molehill or a federal case out of a misdemeanor. We should be mature enough to cast them aside as quickly as they arise.

I wish I could say that all the hurts we receive are minor, but they are not. Many of them are far more serious. Some of the emotional pain we receive is like an open wound; it causes great distress and requires much more than a "bandage" to heal. The pain it inflicts is deep and can be long-lasting.

We cannot pick and choose the problems that we encounter in life, the way we make selections from a menu. Difficult situations *will* occur in our lives. If we fail to cope with these hurts adequately—with the intention of learning and growing from them—they can breed anger, resentment, bitterness, malice, suspicion, distrust, hatred, cynicism, and fear in our lives. They will become like mold that spreads rapidly on a piece of stale bread, destroying both its taste and its ability to be used as food. How effectively we cope with these kinds of hurts will determine our level of growth in the Lord and our emotional health.

Problems are like troubled waters that inevitably crash upon the shores of our lives. As the water rolls up onto the shore, everything in its path is toppled or moved about. Then as it rolls back out to the ocean, it takes with it sand and rocks that formerly seemed to be a permanent part of the shoreline. Similarly, when problems crash upon the shorelines of our lives, and when they retreat again, we are forever changed. Whether that change is good or bad is up to us and our response to our difficulties. Tides are inevitable and necessary to the ebb and flow of ocean life, and problems are necessary and inevitable to the spiritual flow of our lives.

Yet remember that, as a believer in Christ, you are not left to your own resources when you cope with problems. The Scripture promises us, *"And we know that all things work together for good to those who love God, to those who are the called according to His purpose"* (Romans 8:28). Note that this promise is not for everybody. It can be claimed only by those who love God and who are called according to His purpose. *"The called"* are those whom the Holy Spirit has convicted of sin and who have received Christ as their Savior and Lord. Such people have a new perspective, a new mindset, on life. They trust in God and not in life's seeming treasures; they look for their security in Him and not in human resources. They learn to accept—not to resent—pain and persecution, because they know that God is with them at all times to see them through their difficulties. His ultimate goal and purpose is to make us like Christ and to conform us to His image—even through adversity. (See Romans 8:29; 1 John 3:2.) Then as we become more and more like Christ, we will discover our true selves, the people God created us to be. In order to be conformed to Christ's image, you need to

Rx read and heed God's Word.

Rx allow God to teach you through life's struggles.

Rx study Christ's life on earth as your example.

Rx stay filled with God's Spirit.

Rx do God's work in the world.

Follow-Up Visit

Remember, when trouble is not good *to* you, it can still be good *for* you. I look at everything that comes to me as a gift from God—even crises. This Scripture has become my lifeline in times of adversity: *"It is good for me that I have been afflicted, that I may learn Your statutes"* (Psalm 119:71). My prayer is that it will become your lifeline, too.

About the Author

D r. Millicent Hunter is the founder and senior pastor of The Baptist Worship Center in Philadelphia, Pennsylvania. She is also the presiding prelate of the Worship Center Worldwide Fellowship of Churches, which has centers in the United States and South Africa.

Dr. Hunter is the founder of the National Association of Clergy Women, which brings together women in ministry across denominational, racial, and cultural lines, and is a member of the Board of Directors of the Philadelphia Baptist Association. She has an extensive background in education, having served as Dean of the Sanctuary Bible Institute, adjunct professor at various colleges and universities, and cofounder of a school that meets the educational needs of young children from a Christian perspective. Well-known for her exciting and challenging teaching techniques, Dr. Hunter has taught in the Eastern School of Christian Ministry and the Urban Clergy Leadership Institute of Eastern Baptist Theological Seminary.

The award-winning author of several books, Dr. Hunter's first book, *Don't Die in the Winter,* was a best-seller. She has also published numerous articles addressing issues that impact African-American life. Dr. Hunter has received many awards for her involvement in religious and civic affairs, and she was recently included in a pictorial study of African-American life in the twentieth century featured in the Smithsonian Institute.

A mighty, anointed instrument in the hands of an almighty God, the author is a much-sought-after revivalist and conference speaker across the world; she has traveled extensively throughout Japan and Africa, inspiring congregations with messages of hope. She is married to Dr. I. Marino Hunter, and they are the proud parents of two children, Jason and Melissa.

ANOTHER POWERFUL BOOK
from Whitaker House

Loosed to Love
Dr. Rita Twiggs

Today you can be set free and walk right into the powerful things God has for you. Join Dr. Rita Twiggs as she shares how you can break free from the bondages that separate you from the Lover of your soul. You can be released to a new level of intimacy with the Father—a relationship in which you completely trust Him and satisfy Him. Your God-given destiny awaits you. Discover the powerful purpose for your life.

ISBN: 0-88368-651-1 Trade 224 pages

ANOTHER POWERFUL BOOK
from Whitaker House

Imprisoned by Secrets of the Heart
Patricia Harris

That dark secret—the one you buried in the deepest recess of your heart, the one you vowed never to reveal to another living soul, the one that makes you cringe every time it pops into your mind.

Whether it's from hurt, shame, abuse, or fear, we all struggle with inner imprisonment.

Patricia Harris tackles this subject head-on, providing both moving personal accounts and answers to how you can experience a joy-filled new life as you break free from the secrets of your heart.

ISBN: 0-88368-624-4 Trade 192 pages

ANOTHER POWERFUL BOOK
from Whitaker House

Prayer and Fasting
Dr. Kingsley A. Fletcher

Satan is having a field day, diverting the attention of God's people away from their Lord. The enemy of our souls is so afraid of our unused power in God that he is trying to confuse us, individually and collectively. Through fasting and prayer, we can access that unused power and can be victorious.

ISBN: 0-88368-543-4 Trade 168 pages